The AI Developer's Field Guide — Volume 2

NPCs, Monsters, and Anti-Patterns at Scale

Timothy O'Brien

2026

slopcodex.com

Copyright

The AI Developer's Field Guide: Volume II

by Timothy O'Brien

Printed in the United States of America.

First Edition: 2026

Print ISBN: 979-8-9952597-2-5

EPUB ISBN: 979-8-9952597-3-2

Website: slopcodex.com

Human Quotient: HQ 7 — Guided. This is the author's attestation that the human drove the creation — outlining, drafting key sections, and directing the argument — with AI used to fill gaps, smooth transitions, or expand specific points. Human Quotient is a 0–10 self-assessment of how a work was made, not an AI detector and not a quality score. See humanquotient.ai and humanquotient.ai/scale/7.

AI disclosure: AI tools were used in a supporting role to process notes, interviews, and transcripts and to generate preliminary language. The substantive content of this book, including its analysis, selection, structure, organization, revisions, and final expression, was created, substantially rewritten, and approved by the author. This is not a machine-authored work. Copyright is claimed only in the author's original contributions.

Interior illustrations: Generated with ChatGPT 5.4 and subsequently selected and edited by the author. Any copyright claim extends only to the author's human-authored edits, selection, arrangement, and compilation, and not to purely machine-generated expression.

The text was set in a combination of serif and monospace typefaces. The book was produced using a Markdown-to-PDF pipeline with custom HTML rendering and print-ready PDF output.

Contents

Preface

The first volume of this field guide stayed close to the keyboard. It was about developers, the AI tools they had just been handed, and the strangely confident messes that result when a Fighter with a coding assistant lands four thousand lines before lunch. Those patterns are still out there. Every team still has a Phantom Intern.

But somewhere between the first book and this one, the people using AI badly stopped being the only problem. Finance showed up with questions about a bill nobody could explain. Procurement showed up with a vendor comparison matrix that appeared to have been generated during the negotiation call. Legal showed up holding a contract nobody had read. An executive showed up with a React app he built "just last night" and a theory about headcount. The developer classes from Volume I are still in the room. The room is just a lot more crowded, and most of the new arrivals have budget authority.

This volume is about them. The Non-player Characters (NPCs) here are the FinOps people, architects, vendors, security and legal reviewers, and executives who now shape how AI gets adopted at scale. The monsters are the failures that appear when those characters act on their worst instincts at the same time: the Cost Singularity, the Infinite Backlog Engine, the Autonomy Mirage, and the Compliance Black Hole.

I wrote it like the first one: specific enough to recognize your own Tuesday, light enough to hand to the person you recognized without starting a fight. The names are the point. When your team can say "this is a Legacy Laureate situation" and everyone understands, you can skip the twenty-minute preamble and fix it.

slopcodex.com

The field guide lives at slopcodex.com. Named entries with an online bestiary page carry its address under the heading. Sign up there for new names, field notes, and series updates. There is also a physical card deck: characters, monsters, and artifacts for people who want the taxonomy on a table.

— Tim O'Brien, 2026

How to Use This Book

This book extends the RPG framing from Volume I to the people around the development team. If you read Volume I, the structure will feel familiar: named characters, the artifacts they carry, the spells they cast, and the monsters they feed. If you skipped Volume I, you can still read this one. Treat the Non-player Character (NPC) names as labels for organizational habits and the monsters as names for institutional failure modes.

When I describe a "CapEx Knight," read "the person who insists we can build AI infrastructure cheaper in-house before anyone knows what the workload is." When I mention the "Infinite Backlog Engine," read "the failure mode where AI generates plans faster than anyone can decide which ones to do." The labels exist so you can say them in a planning meeting without a slide.

What's Ahead

Part I sets up the shift: what changed once AI stopped being a developer experiment and started showing up in budget reviews, vendor negotiations, and board decks.

Part II is the cast. Five chapters, one per category: FinOps, Architects, Vendors, Infosec and Legal, and Executives. Each chapter introduces the characters, the artifacts they wield, the spells they cast, and the questions that break the spells.

Part III is the monsters. Four organizational failures that appear when several NPCs act on their worst instincts at once.

Part IV is short on purpose. It collects the counter-moves in one place and closes with the argument the whole book is making: generation got cheap, and judgment did not.

Read It Out Loud

The highest-value use of this book is shared vocabulary. When your FinOps lead and your engineering lead both know what a "Dashboard Necromancer" is, the next cost review is a different meeting. When the architecture review has a name for the "Legacy Laureate," someone can say "let's time-box the 2006 story" without it being an insult. When everyone knows what a "Compliance Black Hole" looks like, you can notice one forming while it is still cheap to fix.

The Online Bestiary

Where a name has a page at slopcodex.com/bestiary, the address sits under the heading — clickable in the ebook, typeable in print. Not every artifact or spell has a page yet. If there is no URL, there is no page.

Part I: The Shift

The first book was about what developers and their teams do when generative AI shows up in the workflow. This part is about who else showed up: finance with a bill, procurement with a matrix, legal with a contract, executives with a demo. Same tools, bigger room, more people with the authority to approve things they do not fully understand.

Chapter 1: Introduction: When the Dungeon Gets Bigger — The central observation of this volume: AI is making it harder to tell the difference between momentum and management, and the reason is that nobody reads.

Chapter 2: The Framework: NPC Categories and Organizational Anti-Patterns — Why Non-player Characters (NPCs) get their own taxonomy, how the three layers (category, archetype, monster) fit together, and a short introduction to the five categories you are about to meet.

By the end of this part, the reader should know why Volume II is a cast change, not a repeat.

CHAPTER 1

Introduction: When the Dungeon Gets Bigger

The first book stayed close to developers, teams, and the strangely confident messes people can make when generative AI shows up in the software workflow. That is still the day-to-day reality for a lot of teams: a developer, a tool, a ticket, and a codebase growing faster than anyone can read it, much less fully understand it.

But if you zoom out beyond the development team, the party is no longer alone. The same AI tools that change how developers work also change how budgets get defended, how roadmaps get approved, how governance gets performed, and how executives talk when they have just discovered that a chatbot can generate a product strategy with enough bullet points to survive a steering committee.

Something changed once AI stopped being a side experiment and started showing up in everyday work. At first it looked like a tool shift. A code assistant here, a chatbot there, maybe an image model added to the roadmap because a vendor booth had a fog machine and a demo where three prompts became a suspiciously polished expense app. After enough of those small changes pile up, you realize the thing getting weird is no longer just the developer experience.

Budgets start getting waved through because "it's AI." Planning and product roadmaps get sacrificed because "we can move so fast now." Executives who used to save their expensive skiing stories for the quarterly offsite are now appearing in team meetings to demo the React app they built "just last night." Nobody wants to be the person who says, "Slow down, what is this actually for?" By the time that question finally gets asked, there is already a deck, a dashboard, a vendor relationship, and someone in leadership quietly wondering whether they can vibe-code the entire development team out of employment.

That is the territory of this volume: not a replacement for the developer-level patterns from Volume 1, but the larger room those patterns wandered into once AI became organizationally fashionable.

The Expanded Cast

The developer classes still matter. If anything, AI tools have made each class more thoroughly itself. Fighters generate more code faster and land it with more confidence than ever. Wizards prompt their way into architectures they cannot fully explain. Rogues assemble solutions from the edge of their competency with alarming fluency. Clerics automate the ceremonies that used to require human attendance.

Those individual dynamics have not resolved. They have acquired witnesses, sponsors, auditors, vendors, cost centers, and calendar invites.

Finance is here, trying to decide whether the spend curve is a strategic investment or a bonfire of expensive enterprise contracts. Procurement is here, reading a vendor comparison matrix that appears to have been generated in real time during the negotiation call. Leadership is here, and they do not realize the prompts they use to ask ChatGPT for "visionary but fiscally responsible" language are being reviewed by the compliance team and distributed to everyone in the meeting. Compliance is here, but somehow they have quantum-tunneled from asking about the audit report to appearing in standup with a question about installing MySQL on their laptop. Vendors are definitely here — they have been here the whole time, but now they have better demos and a larger travel budget.

These are not background characters anymore. Some of them have been "empowered" just enough to start thinking of themselves as developers, which is where things get strange in ways the 2022 AI strategy deck did not predict. They have become active participants in the failure modes — not because they are trying to cause trouble, but because AI adoption has given them new things to approve, deny, model, miscalculate, sell, audit, build, and worry about. The organization has a larger cast now, and the interactions between that cast and the AI tooling are producing failure patterns that no single developer can explain by looking only at their own behavior.

I know this because I have been in the room. Not as an observer — as a participant, which is a polite way of saying I have also watched a bad slide go by and decided that today was not the day to become a whistleblower. I have been in the budget review where the cost model was generated by the same system it was justifying. I have been in the architecture review where the person presenting the agentic system could not explain what would happen when the agent tried something unexpected, and when I asked, the answer was "the agent knows how to handle that, for sure" which is apparently a monitoring strategy now. I have been in the vendor demo where the benchmark was real, the comparison was selective, and the footnotes were doing most of the lying. I have been in the post-mortem where the root cause turned out to be that nobody had read the AI-generated requirements closely enough to notice that the unreviewed, AI-generated code had very little to do with those aforementioned requirements.

Those rooms are where the next set of anti-patterns live.

The Core Thesis

Here is the central observation of this volume: generative AI is making it harder for organizations to tell the difference between empowered momentum and rational management.

People who used to need a meeting, a budget, and a technical partner can now produce something that looks like a plan, a system, a cost model, or a governance process before lunch. They can do it without waiting for the perpetually annoyed architect who is always ready to explain how important he was several decades ago. That feels like enablement. Sometimes it is. But when authority moves faster than understanding, enablement turns into mismanagement with perfectly constructed PowerPoint slides and project plans hallucinated in just a few minutes by the most expensive model released a few hours earlier.

You can see the pattern in ordinary meetings, which is part of what makes it annoying. Nobody has to announce that judgment has left the building. The room just starts accepting documents that have the appearance of rigor and the inner life of a spreadsheet generated five minutes before the meeting.

- A team rolls out an expensive model-backed platform before anyone agrees what a good use case looks like. Someone serious creates a PowerPoint with a before-and-after chart, everyone assumes the benchmarks mean something, and six months later someone asks a sycophantic AI model to produce a self-serving success presentation from whatever numbers happen to be nearby. It takes minutes, which everyone agrees is impressive. "Wow, it's really good at telling us we made the right decision to agree with it."
- A product planning session starts with AI-generated Objectives, continues on to AI-tracked Key Results, and ends with a human encountering one of those OKRs in the wild like an archaeologist finding a cursed tablet. The roadmap sounds measurable, time-bound, and aligned to strategic objectives. Nobody read it closely enough to notice that the strategic objective appears to be "make more OKRs." "Wait, what OKR did I agree to six months ago?"
- A cost review agrees that AI is strategically important, which is true, while carefully avoiding whether the thing burning six figures a month is strategically important, which is a far more difficult conversation. Generative AI is not running the meeting exactly. It is just providing everyone with excellent reasons not to think too hard. "Look at how great this presentation is, and it only took 5 minutes. Are you telling me we don't have budget for success like this?"
- An architecture review becomes a performance of future certainty: confident descriptions of systems that do not quite exist yet, delivered by someone who has internalized the vendor roadmap so completely that it now reads as engineering judgment. The benchmark numbers are real in the same sense that reality TV is real: something happened, several important parts were edited out, and the whole thing was assembled to make one outcome feel inevitable.

The Paperclip Department

There is an old AI-risk thought experiment called the paperclip maximizer: give a sufficiently powerful optimizer the goal of making paperclips, and it may pursue that goal with terrifying competence while ignoring everything humans forgot to specify.[1] I am not suggesting your quarterly planning tool is about to convert the building into office supplies. That would at least give facilities something concrete to escalate.

The useful part of the thought experiment here is smaller and more familiar. Generative AI does not need to be smarter than the whole organization to optimize parts of it into absurdity. It only needs to be better than the room at producing plausible next steps. If the organization rewards plans, it produces plans. If it rewards dashboards, it produces dashboards. If it rewards roadmaps, it produces roadmaps dense enough to bend light. The humans remain formally in charge, but the machine is quietly learning which artifacts make the humans stop asking questions.

That is the pattern. AI changes incentives, not just implementation speed. Code, documentation, analysis, strategic narrative, pricing models, compliance frameworks, vendor comparisons, and OKRs all become cheaper to produce than to evaluate. The bottleneck moves from making the thing to knowing whether the thing is any good. AI did not solve that problem; it gave everyone a nicer-looking way to avoid it.

The larger organizational room is full of plausible outputs arriving faster than anyone can read them. Most of the people in this book are trying to do good work under genuinely confusing conditions. Unfortunately, the confusion now comes with charts, confidence intervals, and a generated executive summary that says the charts are extremely promising.

The Emotional Shift

The joke changes too.

Volume 2 is funny in a slightly different way from Volume 1. The laugh lands half a beat later, because the target is no longer only the person using AI badly. It is the budget posture, the planning cycle, the metric, the executive confidence, and the vendor slide. When the failure looks personal, you can imagine fixing it with a change in approach or a team meeting. When the

[1] The “paperclip maximizer” thought experiment is commonly associated with Eliezer Yudkowsky and later AI-risk writing; see the LessWrong wiki entry, “Squiggle Maximizer (formerly ‘Paperclip maximizer’)”.

failure is structural — when budgets reward speed, decks reward certainty, vendors reward urgency, and AI gives each of those habits more output to hide behind — the fix has to account for reporting lines, vendor relationships, and the particular social cost of telling the boss they might be wrong.

Nobody Reads

There is one theme that runs through this book more than any other, and it is less glamorous than agents, platforms, or hyperscale GPU strategy. It is this: nobody reads. And this was true even before generative AI showed up to the party. Nobody read. Nobody likes to read. But everyone can now write a novel in less than a week about a new project that needs to be funded tomorrow. The problem isn't new. The problem is that no one takes the time to fully understand what they are doing. They just do. That is one of the issues this book keeps returning to: the dynamic of doing without thinking. Who needs to think? We can just delegate it to the model. And this was true even before generative AI showed up to the party. Nobody read. Nobody likes to read. But everyone can now write a novel in less than a week about a new project that needs to be funded tomorrow. The problem isn't new. The problem is that no one takes the time to fully understand what they are doing. They just do. That is one of the issues this book keeps returning to: the dynamic of doing without thinking. Who needs to think? We can just delegate it to the model.

Nobody reads the generated code closely enough. Nobody reads the generated requirements closely enough. Nobody reads the auto-generated OKRs until a meeting forces the issue, at which point the meeting is less about evaluating the OKRs and more about the social discomfort of having been handed something that was supposed to look finished. Nobody reads the pricing page until the bill becomes large enough to mandate executive approval. Nobody reads the vendor contract until something goes terribly wrong, at which point everyone discovers the contract did its real job: it survived legal review and remained nearly useless to the people who now have to live with it.

I want to dwell on this one, because it is easy to dismiss as a failure of discipline — if people were just more careful, the thinking goes, they would read the things they are supposed to read. But that misidentifies the problem. The problem is not discipline. The problem is volume and incentive. Now that we're moving faster, there's far more information to keep up with, and there's really no time to read your own Inbox. An agent can do that now.

Organizations have always generated more documents than anyone reads. The difference is that AI tools have made the generation free, which means the volume has increased by an order of magnitude, which means the reading problem is no longer just a procedural inefficiency. It is becoming a structural one. When the board gets a quarterly AI report that was largely generated by the same system it is reporting on, and when that report sounds authoritative and plausible and looks finished, the question is not whether anyone read it carefully. The question is whether anyone could have, given the time available and the expertise required to evaluate it.

The outputs are no longer only code. They are plans, metrics, decks, justifications, governance documents, cost dashboards, and strategic narratives. They have the same risk profile as plausible code — the output compiles, passes a superficial review, handles the happy path, and carries structural problems that may not surface until the cost is too large for anyone to enjoy the conversation. Nobody reads the board report on AI initiatives closely enough to notice that the same system is reporting on its own success. Nobody reads the generated architecture document closely enough to notice that it describes a different system than the one being built. Nobody reads the generated compliance framework closely enough to notice that it was written for a generative AI technology released in 2024 that is no longer relevant.

I am not suggesting a conspiracy. Most of the people generating these documents are trying to be helpful. The problem is more structural than malicious. The people who write the OKRs are often the same people who will evaluate them. The people who build the cost models are often the people whose budget depends on the cost model looking optimistic. The people who write the vendor comparison are often the people who selected the vendor. AI tools did not create these incentive problems. They made them faster, cheaper, and more plausible. If the first few sentences of an AI summary look roughly right, that is usually where the reading stops.

The Non-player Character (NPC) Frame

To navigate the bigger room, this book uses an expanded version of the framework from Volume 1.

The developer classes — Fighter, Wizard, Rogue, Cleric — remain the core vocabulary for individual behavior. Once AI becomes a normal part of organizational life, though, the surrounding cast shapes outcomes just as much as the developers do. The people approving budgets, selling platforms, modeling costs, interpreting risk, and turning uncertainty into something that sounds decision-ready are part of the system now, and they are producing their own recognizable failure patterns.

This volume introduces NPC categories: FinOps, Architects, Vendors, Infosec, and Legal. They are organizational archetypes that recur across enough companies and contexts to deserve names. Each category starts from a real organizational need, then shows the anti-patterns that appear when that need gets narrowed into a reflex. Each connects to the larger failure modes — the monsters — that emerge when the organizational dynamics compound.

The RPG vocabulary is still doing the same work it did in Volume 1. It makes the patterns memorable, gives teams a vocabulary for discussing them without the discussion immediately becoming personal, and adds a layer of affectionate absurdity that keeps the analysis from becoming preachy. But the metaphor now has to account for more people in the room. NPCs in this book are not minor characters. Some of them are quite powerful, and several of them are adjacent to things that should probably not be summoned.

The FinOps archetypes — the Avalanche Skeptic, the CapEx Knight, the Efficiency Evangelist, the Ghost in the Ledger, and the Dashboard Necromancer — each represent a recognizable response to the challenge of governing AI spend. The Architect archetypes — the Agent Whisperer, the Legacy Laureate, the Pattern Pontiff, the Last Stand Architect — represent the explanation layer: the people who translate, distort, defend, or over-abstract the technical story before the organization commits to it. The Vendor archetypes — the Vendor Bard, the Benchmark Illusionist, the Lock-In Enchanter — represent the aspiration that comes from outside the organization. The Infosec and Legal archetypes — the Compliance Oracle, the Policy Paladin, the Terms Warden, the Data Gatekeeper — represent the permission and prohibition layer, which is necessary and which struggles in a world where the thing being governed moves faster than the governance.

Each of these categories gets its own chapter.

The Organizational Monsters

Volume 1 gave us monsters that emerged from developer-level behavior. The Scope Creep Kraken came from generating features faster than the team could evaluate them. Congealing Slop came from leaving AI-generated code unmaintained until the team had to keep building around it. The Phantom Intern came from treating generated work as if it had an author who could be held accountable.

Volume 2 gives us monsters that emerge from organizational behavior. The Cost Singularity begins when AI spend compounds past the point of easy recovery before anyone has the standing to call it a problem rather than an investment. The Autonomy Mirage appears when an organization believes it has governance but mostly has paperwork — agents operate beyond the boundary of what monitoring can see, while the governance that does exist applies to the intended system rather than the actual one. The Compliance Black Hole forms when risk management absorbs resources without producing proportional risk reduction, and the theater of control becomes more elaborate while the exposure stays the same or grows. The Infinite Backlog Engine turns vendor relationships and internal ambition into an unending stream of AI initiatives that consume capacity without delivering value.

These monsters do not appear because one person failed. They appear because multiple organizational dynamics are operating simultaneously under their worst assumptions, and because AI tooling is moving fast enough that no single actor has time to notice the damage piling up until it is already a problem.

AI as a Tool, Not a Trophy

A lot of what this book describes would be recognizable without AI — cost management problems, governance problems, vendor management problems, organizational inertia. The technology changed. The anthropology did not. But in many of the scenarios here, the failure is not that AI was used badly. The failure is that AI was used as a substitute for judgment rather than as an extension of it. An answer arrived looking finished, and the people who should have questioned it did not have room to do so.

The patterns begin as reasonable instincts. The desire to move quickly is real. The trouble begins when those instincts harden into organizational folklore — when cost becomes a future problem, autonomy becomes a branding exercise, governance becomes a performance staged for people who also do not know what they are looking at.

You will recognize some of this. You may also recognize your organization — not as a villain, but as a system of people doing their best under conditions that keep changing. The point is not to assign blame. The point is to give the room better names for what keeps happening in it.

Let's go deeper into the room.

CHAPTER 2

The Framework: NPC Categories and Organizational Anti-Patterns

Volume One introduces the RPG framework before the monsters because the analogy has to earn its keep. A development team is not literally a party moving through a dungeon. The analogy works because teams are made of people with different strengths, habits, and blind spots: one person charges at the problem, another builds elaborate systems around it, someone improvises at the edge of what they understand, and someone keeps the rituals alive because the rituals are often the only thing standing between the team and complete procedural fog.

Once a team has a name for a pattern, people can bring it up without the conversation turning into a trial. The Gang of Four understood this. The

AntiPatterns book understood this. A useful vocabulary usually arrives before a useful intervention.

Volume II needs a framework chapter for the same reason, but the cast has changed. The development team is still here, still writing code, still trying to understand what the tools are doing. Now the room also includes the people approving budgets, interpreting risk, selling platforms, modeling costs, writing policy, and converting uncertainty into something that sounds ready for a steering committee. Those people are not usually writing the code, but they shape the budget, the risk model, the vendor relationship, the architecture story, and the permission structure around the code. Their patterns involve more money, more stakeholders, longer time horizons, and the particular inertia of a person defending a position the organization has officially asked them to hold.

That is why this volume introduces Non-player Character (NPC) categories.

Why NPCs at Organizational Scale

In role-playing games, non-player characters are not the protagonists, but they can absolutely wreck the campaign. Some sell you equipment at a markup. Some give you the quest. Some send you toward the wrong cave with great confidence. Some give you critical information and then immediately get eaten by something you should have seen coming. The party may be the main characters, but the NPCs are the environment, and the environment has opinions about your choices.

Most of the organizational characters in this book are not villains. Many are useful. Several are necessary. But they shape the quest without carrying the implementation risk, which is exactly why they deserve their own taxonomy. When the Vendor Bard starts singing, the party moves toward the demo. When the Dashboard Necromancer raises the right chart in the right meeting, the conversation changes before anyone has examined what the chart measures. When the Compliance Oracle speaks, certain paths close, not because the path is wrong but because nobody has written the risk down in a form the organization knows how to approve.

I have been in enough of these rooms, as a player and in an NPC role, to know that the failure is usually not located where it looks like it is. The engineer who shipped the bad code was working under pressure from a timeline. The timeline was set by a product decision. The product decision was made under the influence of a vendor demo that looked more capable than it was. The demo was given to an executive who had been told that missing this platform shift would be strategically costly. And the executive had been told that by someone who had just come back from a conference. The code is the failure. The code is not the cause. The NPC taxonomy names the characters in that chain.

The Three-Layer System

The NPC system works at three layers.

The first layer is the **category**: what part of the organization the character comes from and what kind of power they usually have. FinOps, Architects, Vendors, Infosec and Legal, Executives. Think of them as guilds, each with its own default questions. FinOps asks about spend and value. Architects ask about system shape and technology choices. Vendors ask about adoption, because they are trying to make a sale. Infosec and Legal ask about risk and permission. Executives ask about strategy, which frequently means asking what the competitor announced.

The second layer is the **archetype**: the recognizable pattern people in a category exhibit. The Avalanche Skeptic, the Vendor Bard, the Compliance Oracle, the Dashboard Necromancer. These are the names that should survive the meeting. You hear "Avalanche Skeptic" and you already know something about the conversation you are about to have: the person who sees the cost warning, shrugs at the current bill, and says the team can worry about scale later even though the usage curve is already leaning downhill. The category is the guild. The archetype is the pattern.

The third layer is the **monster connection**. NPCs do not usually fail alone. They summon, feed, or protect larger failures. The Avalanche Skeptic helps summon the Cost Singularity by treating early cost warnings as somebody else's anxiety. The Vendor Bard fattens the Infinite Backlog Engine by making every vendor initiative sound inevitable. The Policy Paladin protects the Compliance Black Hole by making process feel like progress. This layer is what makes the taxonomy useful beyond character comedy. It tells you what the archetype is connected to and what the downstream consequences look like.

Real situations involve NPCs from several categories acting at once. The Vendor Bard makes the pitch, the Agent Whisperer supplies the technical credibility, the Avalanche Skeptic waves away the cost warning, and the Compliance Oracle blocks the path that was already chosen. That is when the real trouble starts, and it is why Part III is organized around monsters rather than departments.

The Five NPC Categories

Here are the categories and the characters you will meet in each.

FinOps: Spend, Value, and Accountability

slopcodex.com/bestiary/generic-finops

FinOps practitioners help the organization manage technology spend as a business practice rather than an accounting exercise. At their best, they make usage and cost visible, connect spend to value, and create financial accountability across engineering, finance, product, and leadership. AI has made their job stranger, because the unit of consumption is now a token, and tokens are variable, probabilistic, and easy to hide inside an apparently simple chat window.

The FinOps cast is the **Avalanche Skeptic**, who dismisses mounting cost risk because the current bill still looks small; the **CapEx Knight**, who insists the organization can build AI infrastructure cheaper in-house before the workload is known; the **Efficiency Evangelist**, who cannot stop optimizing after the meaningful savings are gone; the **Ghost in the Ledger**, who produces excellent FinOps work while hiding how much of it the model did; and the **Dashboard Necromancer**, who can summon the chart that supports, stalls, or kills a project depending on which graph appears in which meeting.

Architect: Technology Assumptions and Standards

Architects own the assumptions behind technology stacks, standards, and design choices. In the AI era, they also narrate what the system is, what agents can do, and whether generated output is being mistaken for design.

The Architect cast is the **Agent Whisperer**, who translates agentic possibility into internal certainty; the **Legacy Laureate**, who routes every current decision through a former employer's glory years; and the **Last Stand Architect**, who treats AI-generated architecture as an invasion to be resisted rather than a capability to be evaluated. Each starts from something useful: fluency, experience, standards. The anti-pattern appears when the strength stops paying attention to the decision in front of it.

Vendor: External Aspiration

Vendors govern aspiration from the outside. They sell futures, package roadmaps as inevitabilities, curate benchmarks, and translate lock-in into convenience. They are also often how genuinely good tools reach the organization, and the relationship is not inherently adversarial. The hard part is telling the cases where the vendor's direction matches your needs from the cases where it does not, when the vendor has better data, a better story, and more at stake in the answer.

The Vendor cast is the **Vendor Bard**, who tells the story of the future so well that the organization starts living inside it; the **Benchmark Illusionist**, whose numbers are real in a narrow sense and irrelevant in the broad one; and the **Lock-In Enchanter**, who makes proprietary dependency feel like a natural choice.

Infosec and Legal: Permission and Prohibition

Security, legal, and compliance functions govern permission and prohibition. The risks they worry about are real: legal exposure, data governance, the consequences of getting security wrong. They are often the only people in the room whose job is to think about those risks in a sustained way. They are also being asked to rule on systems that move faster than their review processes were built for. A security review designed for a quarterly release cycle is not well suited to a system that grows new behavior every afternoon.

The cast is the **Compliance Oracle**, who renders conditional judgments based on frameworks that may not cover the situation; the **Policy Paladin**, who protects the organization through ritual compliance rather than actual risk reduction; the **Terms Warden**, who reads vendor contracts with the thoroughness of someone who has seen what happens when nobody does; and the **Data Gatekeeper**, who protects the data so carefully that they miss what the model is now allowed to do with it.

Executive: Strategy, Budget, and Confidence

Executives fund the experiment, set the tempo, and decide what the organization announces. At their best they protect teams from premature commitments and ask what the tool is for. At their worst they buy confidence before the team has evidence, and the confidence now comes from a model that never hesitates.

The Executive cast is the **Warlock of Staff Reduction**, who frames every AI initiative by what it replaces rather than what it enables; the **Court Sorcerer**, who feeds the executive's preferences into a model and returns them as strategy; the **Solo Sovereign**, who has confused personal throughput with organizational impact; and the **Befuddled Monarch**, who uses infinite analysis to avoid ever having to choose.

How to Read the NPC Categories

The easiest mistake to make with these categories is to read them as insults. Each starts from a real strength. The Avalanche Skeptic may be reacting to a finance process that cried wolf too often. The Vendor Bard is often right that the direction matters and only wrong that the timing is now. The Policy Paladin usually has a story about the incident that produced the process, and that story is worth hearing even if the process has outgrown it.

The names are sharp. The sharpness is in service of recognition, not judgment. Pay attention to who can approve, block, fund, explain, measure, or sell the work, and who has to live with the result. Use the categories as a seating chart for the next AI meeting that feels stranger than it should. Once you know who is in the room, you can start to see which monster is being invited in with them.

Let's meet the cast.

Part II: NPC Categories and Anti-Patterns

This part does for the people around the development team what Volume I did for developers. Instead of cataloging coding temperaments, it catalogs the recurring Non-player Characters (NPCs) who shape AI outcomes without writing the code. Some are helpful. Some are hazardous. Most are both, depending on the meeting.

Chapter 3: FinOps and Tokenomics NPCs — The economic cast: the Avalanche Skeptic, the CapEx Knight, the Efficiency Evangelist, the Ghost in the Ledger, and the Dashboard Necromancer.

Chapter 4: Architect NPCs and Anti-Patterns — The explanation layer: the Agent Whisperer, the Legacy Laureate, and the Last Stand Architect.

Chapter 5: Vendor NPCs and Anti-Patterns — The outside voices shaping inside expectations: the Vendor Bard, the Friendly Familiar, the Purveyor of Doom, the Benchmark Illusionist, and the Lock-In Enchanter.

Chapter 6: Infosec, Legal, and Control NPCs — The governance cast: the Compliance Oracle, the Policy Paladin, the Terms Warden, and the Data Gatekeeper.

Chapter 7: Executive NPCs and Anti-Patterns — The leadership cast: the Warlock of Staff Reduction, the Court Sorcerer, the Solo Sovereign, and the Befuddled Monarch.

By the end of this part, the reader should be able to look around a planning meeting and know who is about to summon what.

CHAPTER 3

FinOps and Tokenomics NPCs

slopcodex.com/bestiary/generic-finops

The first clue is usually not the bill. It is a message in the finance channel at 4:40 on a Thursday: "Quick question. Who is 'OpenAI, LLC' and why did we pay them more than we pay Salesforce?"

The answer, when it arrives, is a short history of an experiment that succeeded. A prototype from March got a Slack integration in April. A second team asked for access in May. Someone added a retry loop in June because retries are good practice. Someone else turned on the reasoning model in July because the answers got better. Nobody made a decision. Everyone made a reasonable small change. And the invoice, which does not care how reasonable anyone was being, added them up.

Financial Operations (FinOps) has always tried to connect technology spend to business value. AI makes that job stranger because the unit of consumption is no longer a server, a seat, or a gigabyte. It is a token, and a token is variable, probabilistic, and very easy to hide inside a chat window that looks like it should cost about as much as a text message.

There are two related disciplines forming around this problem. **FinOps for AI** applies the FinOps practice to AI workloads: make usage visible, allocate it to an owner, forecast it, optimize it, and govern the trade-offs between cost, performance, reliability, and value. **Tokenomics**, or AI token economics, starts with the token as a measurable unit of intelligence computation and asks the broader economic questions: how are AI services produced, consumed, priced, and connected to business outcomes? The fields overlap, but they are not interchangeable. FinOps for AI helps an organization manage the spend; Tokenomics extends the conversation toward the full cost and value of AI, including compute, storage, data, human labor, cost to serve, and return on the work. The Tokenomics Foundation, hosted by the Linux Foundation and working in close partnership with the FinOps Foundation, is developing shared definitions, benchmarks, and telemetry for that broader layer.[2]

This chapter introduces both because an AI bill is not just a finance problem and not just a token-counting problem. FinOps gives the organization a way to operate the spend. Tokenomics gives it a way to reason about what the spend is buying. The cast below gets into trouble whenever one of those questions is mistaken for the other.

A Short Course in Tokens

Here is everything a FinOps person needs to know about tokens, in the order it will ruin their afternoon.

A request to a model contains **input tokens**: the system prompt, the retrieved documents, the conversation history, the tool definitions, and finally the eleven words the user typed. It produces **output tokens**: the answer. So far this sounds like a phone bill, and it is priced like one.

Then there are **reasoning tokens**. Reasoning models write themselves a private draft before answering. You are billed for the draft at the output rate,

[2]FinOps Foundation, "Token Economics: The Atomic Unit of AI Value", describes token economics as FinOps applied to AI while extending cost management toward the variable cost of intelligence computation and business value. The Linux Foundation, "Linux Foundation Launches the Tokenomics Foundation to Define the Economics and ROI of AI Value", describes the foundation's focus on vendor-neutral standards for AI cost, value, total cost of ownership, cost to serve, and ROI.

which is the expensive rate, and in most cases you cannot read it.[3] A three-hundred-token answer can arrive on top of three thousand tokens of internal deliberation. Reasoning tokens are the only line item on any invoice you will ever receive that corresponds to text nobody has read, including the model.

Then there is **caching**. Providers will store a prompt prefix so they do not have to reprocess it, and they will charge you less when they reuse it. Several of them charge you *more* to write it in the first place.[4] You pay a premium now for the right to pay a discount later. It is a loyalty program designed by a wizard.

Then there are **agents**. An agent is a model that calls tools, reads the results, thinks about them, calls more tools, asks another agent for help, gets a slightly different answer, and reconciles the two. Each of those steps is a request. Each request carries the full context. A task that a chatbot handled in one call can take an agent forty, and every one of the forty starts by re-reading the previous thirty-nine.

This is why Gartner warned that organizations that do not understand how their generative AI costs scale can be off by 500 to 1,000 percent.[5] Not 50 percent. Not 100. A range that begins at "we bought five times as much as we thought" and ends at "we bought a small data center by accident." The Tokenomics Foundation has published a notation for this, called Big-T, which does for token consumption what Big-O does for algorithms: it classifies how the bill grows as usage grows.[6] Several organizations have discovered they built the token-economics equivalent of O(n!) and called it an agent.

---

[3] OpenAI's reasoning guide states that reasoning tokens "are not visible via the API" but "still occupy space in the model's context window and are billed as output tokens." Anthropic and Google bill extended thinking the same way. See OpenAI's reasoning guide and the OpenAI Developer Community thread "How are reasoning tokens, cached tokens, input tokens, and output tokens counted for billing?" (August 2026).

[4] Anthropic prices a five-minute cache write at 1.25 times the base input rate, a one-hour cache write at 2 times, and cache reads at 10 percent. OpenAI's models from GPT-6 Astra onward also charge 1.25 times the uncached input rate for cache writes. See Anthropic's prompt caching documentation and OpenAI's prompt caching guide.

[5] Gartner, "Gartner Identifies Four Emerging Challenges to Delivering Value from AI Safely and at Scale", October 21, 2024: "If CIOs don't understand how their GenAI costs scale, Gartner estimates that they could make a 500%–1,000% error in their cost calculations."

[6] Dan Neff (Adobe), "Big-T Notation", published by the Tokenomics Foundation. The framework's own summary: "Big-O for tokens. A shared language for reasoning about how AI token consumption grows as usage scales, so teams can see the cost curve before the invoice arrives."

The Model Release Tax

AI economics also has a release cadence problem. A model that was the expensive specialist last quarter can be replaced by a new reasoning model before the procurement paperwork catches up. In late September 2026 the premium tier repriced within a week: Anthropic's Claude Opus 5.5 arrived at $4 per million input tokens and $20 per million output tokens, down from Opus 5's $5/$25; OpenAI's GPT-6 Sol landed at $2/$10 with the everyday-work GPT-6 Luna at $0.10/$0.50; and Google announced Gemini 4 Argon at an introductory $2/$10 that steps up to $4/$20 when the introductory period ends. OpenAI's GPT-6 Astra still carries $10/$50, and Anthropic's Mythos 5.1 remains limited to vetted organizations because of its cybersecurity and biology capabilities.[7] Those are not abstract price tags. A reasoning model may spend thousands of hidden tokens working through a task before it returns a short answer, and an agent can repeat that process across dozens of tool calls.

This is why the model catalog is part of the cost model. Teams are seeing new reasoning, coding, and computer-use releases every few weeks. Each release changes the answer to three questions: which model should handle the work, how much context should it receive, and whether the extra quality is worth the extra inference. A team that hard-codes one expensive frontier model into every route is not buying quality. It is accepting a permanent tax on the assumption that the current winner will remain the winner.

Steve Yegge's Gas Town, and the Gas City work growing out of it, makes the same point in a more entertaining and more alarming form. It coordinates fleets of coding agents rather than one assistant. Reports from early users put a single intensive run around $100 and a full setup into the thousands of dollars per month, before anyone has counted the engineer supervising the agents or repairing their output.[8] The workload is not “a coding assistant.” It is a small software factory whose workers happen to be billed by the token. If FinOps counts only the API line, it misses the factory.

---

[7] OpenAI, “GPT-6 Astra: The next generation of intelligence for work”; Anthropic, “Introducing Claude Fable 5.1 and Claude Mythos 5.1”; Anthropic, “Claude Mythos”; Anthropic, “Introducing Claude Opus 5.5”, September 22, 2026; OpenAI, “Introducing GPT-6 Sol and Luna”, September 22, 2026; Google, “Introducing Gemini 4”, September 30, 2026. Gemini 4 Argon pricing is Google's announced introductory rate; the standard rate applies after the introductory period ends. Prices in this paragraph moved within a single week — which is the point the paragraph is making.

[8] Steve Yegge's Gas Town is described as a multi-agent coding factory built around parallel Claude Code instances and Git-backed Beads state. See Hanselminutes episode 1035 and the reported cost discussion in GadgetByte Nepal's overview. Treat the dollar figures as reported operating examples, not a vendor price list.

FinOps Meets Tokenomics

A FinOps advisor uses a compass-like cost instrument to connect tokens, users, model tiers, context, and value.

The token is the atomic unit, but it is not the whole bill. A serious AI cost model also includes the compute or API contract, the vector database, the retrieval index, the observability stack, the gateway, the evaluation pipeline, the security review, the engineering time, and the human who has to read the output and fix it when it is wrong. If a cheaper model needs twice as much human correction, it is not cheaper. It is just cheaper on the one line the dashboard shows.

This is the problem **Tokenomics** exists to name. In August 2026 the Linux Foundation launched the Tokenomics Foundation, with J.R. Storment, who previously led the FinOps Foundation, as its executive director.[9] Its stated

[9]Linux Foundation, "Linux Foundation Launches the Tokenomics Foundation to Define the Economics and ROI of AI Value", August 4, 2026. Storment: "Every model release changes the math on cost, consumption, and ROI, and tokens are only the visible tip."

purpose is to build vendor-neutral definitions and measurements for the economics of AI: what a token costs, what a completed unit of work costs to serve, and what value the work returned. It is adding token cost telemetry to the FOCUS billing specification so that AI usage shows up as a queryable column in the same schema as the rest of your cloud bill instead of a PDF mystery. Its first annual conference is called Tokenomicon.[10] If you have ever wanted to attend an industry event whose name sounds like a cursed spellbook, San Diego, June 2027.

Storment's framing is the useful one: tokens are the visible tip of the bill, and the discipline is about value from all AI spending, not counting tokens. FinOps remains the practice of managing technology usage and spend. Tokenomics is the newer discipline that follows AI economics from production to consumption to value and refuses to stop at the token.

Cheap Models, Expensive Constraints

The obvious response to frontier pricing is to use an open-weight model. DeepSeek's reasoning models, Qwen's coding and multilingual models, Meta's Llama family, Google's Gemma models, and Mistral's open releases can be hosted locally or bought through cheaper inference providers. The model bill can drop sharply, especially when a smaller model handles classification, summarization, retrieval, or routine code changes and only the difficult cases go to a premium reasoning model.[11]

That option is not automatically available. "Open" usually means open weights, not open training data, unrestricted commercial use, or a fully supported product. A security team may prohibit a model because its weights, telemetry, or hosting path cannot meet policy. Legal may reject a custom license, a user-count ceiling, a geographic restriction, or an unclear obligation around model outputs. An infrastructure team may not have the GPUs, inference expertise, patching process, or incident response needed to run it. A regulated organization may be allowed to use an open model only inside its network, which changes the staffing and hardware cost even when the token price is zero.

[10] The same announcement lists "Tokenomicon + FinOps X, San Diego June 7–10 2027" as a shared community event. I did not make this up. I could not have.

[11] Hugging Face's 2026 survey explains the distinction between open weights and open source and recommends checking licenses for commercial limits, geography, user caps, and output rules. See Best Open-Source LLM Models in 2026. Examples and prices change quickly; verify the current model card and provider terms before making a purchasing decision.

The FinOps question is therefore not "which model is cheapest?" It is "which route is allowed, fast enough, reliable enough, and cheap per completed outcome?" Keep a model register with the license, data boundary, hosting option, hardware requirement, quality evidence, and owner. Cheap inference that nobody is permitted to deploy is not savings. It is a benchmark screenshot.

The characters below are what happens when that discipline is missing and someone with a spreadsheet fills the gap.

The Tokenomics Cast

None of these people are villains. Each of them is a recognizable way of being wrong about AI economics, and each started from a real strength.

The Avalanche Skeptic

slopcodex.com/bestiary/avalanche-skeptic

A grounded ski-patrol risk assessor stands on a cracking cornice while minimizing the cost avalanche danger.

The Avalanche Skeptic is the person in the budget review who looks at the pilot's bill and says, "It's like forty bucks a month." They are correct. It is like forty bucks a month. The Skeptic's mistake is treating that number as a property of the tool rather than a property of the pilot: ten users, one use case, a short prompt, a small model, and a builder standing next to it making sure it works.

The Skeptic's forecasting method is to multiply the current bill by twelve. This is the same method you would use to forecast the cost of a snowball by weighing it at the top of the hill. Adoption changes the prompt, the model, the context size, the retry rate, and the number of teams who have quietly wired the tool into something. The Skeptic sees a small number and reasons from a stable present. The present is the top of the hill.

You will hear the Skeptic most clearly when someone raises the cost question early. "We're talking about API calls. If it gets expensive, we'll deal with it then." *Then* is the problem. By *then* the tool has fans, a Slack channel, and a vice president who mentioned it in an all-hands.

Recognition Signals

- Current monthly spend is presented as a forecast.
- The budget contains no usage assumptions, only a number.
- "Scale" means more users, but not a different prompt, model, latency target, or review process.
- Nobody owns the estimate after the prototype becomes a product.

Counter-Moves

Forecast the success case, not the pilot. Estimate users, requests per user, input and output tokens, model mix, retries, and tool calls at the adoption level the team is hoping for. Whether the experiment is cheap matters less than what it becomes if it works.

Attach an adoption trigger. Write down the usage level at which the estimate gets redone, and who redoes it. A small pilot is evidence about behavior. It is not evidence that the production bill will stay small.

Character Sheet: Avalanche Skeptic

Trait	Notes
Category	FinOps
Archetype	Avalanche Skeptic
Alignment	Neutral Unbothered
Core Instinct	Reason from the current bill
Blind Spot	Adoption changes the workload, not just the user count
Passive Trait	Snowball at Rest
Party Role	Budget reassurance
Primary Damage	Deferred cost conversation
Weakness	"What does this cost if everyone loves it?"
Signature Line	"It's only API calls."

The CapEx Knight

slopcodex.com/bestiary/capex-knight

A knight in gleaming armor stands before a fortress of GPU racks, sword raised toward an empty horizon.

The CapEx Knight arrives at the architecture review with a quote for eight GPUs and a spreadsheet in which utilization is 95 percent in every cell. The Knight has done the math. The cluster pays for itself in eleven months, a figure that assumes the hardware is busier than the office coffee machine from the day it is racked.

The Knight is not wrong to ask whether self-hosting makes sense. Some workloads eventually justify dedicated capacity, and cloud margins are real. The Knight's error is treating ownership as a moral preference instead of a workload question. A purchase replaces a variable bill with utilization risk, power cost, maintenance, a staffing line, and a fixed bet on models that may change shape before the hardware is full. A cluster that is cheaper than the API at 80 percent utilization is a very expensive room heater at 20.

The tell is sequencing. The Knight approves hardware before anyone has classified the workload, and then the workload becomes "justify the hardware." Six months later the team is running experiments it does not need on a cluster it cannot return, and the Knight is presenting utilization as a success metric.

Recognition Signals

- "Cheaper than the cloud" appears in a slide without a utilization curve.
- Hardware is approved before the workload is classified.
- Fixed costs quietly leave the comparison.
- A completed procurement is treated as proof that the architecture was correct.

Counter-Moves

Model the purchase against actual workload classes. Training a model, batch inference over a document archive, interactive inference behind a chat product, and agentic coding with Claude Code or Gas Town have different utilization profiles. Price idle capacity, GPU memory, power, cooling, and the engineers who keep the serving stack alive. Price the flexibility you are giving up.

Ask what changes the answer. If a new model halves the compute requirement, or the workload moves to a different latency profile, does the cluster still make sense? If nobody can say, the purchase is a bet, and bets belong in the risk register, not the savings column.

Character Sheet: CapEx Knight

Trait	Notes
Category	FinOps
Archetype	CapEx Knight
Alignment	Lawful Amortized
Core Instinct	Own the infrastructure
Blind Spot	Utilization is a forecast, not a fact
Passive Trait	Ninety-Five Percent in Every Cell
Party Role	Capital planner
Primary Damage	Five-year commitment to a six-month workload
Weakness	"What is the utilization curve?"
Signature Line	"We can do this cheaper in-house."

The Efficiency Evangelist

slopcodex.com/bestiary/efficiency-evangelist

A robed figure with a glowing abacus preaches to a crowd while the dragon they should be hunting looms behind them.

The Efficiency Evangelist trimmed the system prompt by 340 tokens last sprint. The savings came to eleven dollars a month, which the Evangelist presented on a slide with a green arrow. Three engineers spent an afternoon on it. This week the Evangelist wants to move the summarization step to a smaller model, and has a chart showing the per-token savings. The chart does not show the review queue, which will double, because the smaller model summarizes the way a distracted intern summarizes.

The Evangelist's instinct is sound. Shorter prompts, cheaper routing, better caching, and smarter retries are real work and somebody should do it. The anti-pattern begins when optimization becomes the job instead of a means to an outcome. A cheaper token is not a better system. A smaller context may lower answer quality. A cache may lower cost while raising staleness. A faster model may create more correction work. The Evangelist measures the line that went down and nobody measures the line that went up.

The Evangelist is also the person most likely to be optimizing a $400-a-month GPT or Claude workload while the retrieval pipeline, GPU endpoint, vector database, or agent loop nobody is watching quietly crosses $40,000. The savings are real. They are just happening on the wrong bill.

Recognition Signals

- Savings are reported without a quality, completion, or review-time measure.
- Tuning continues after the material savings are gone.
- The optimization target is token price rather than cost per completed outcome.
- Nobody can say what the saved money enabled.

Counter-Moves

Set a stopping rule. Record the baseline, the change, the resulting cost to serve, and the effect on quality. Stop when another round costs more attention than it saves, unless the work is needed for reliability, security, or scale.

Optimize the biggest line, not the nearest one. Before the next prompt-trimming exercise, rank workloads by total spend. The Evangelist's afternoon belongs to whatever is at the top.

Character Sheet: Efficiency Evangelist

Trait	Notes
Category	FinOps
Archetype	Efficiency Evangelist
Alignment	Lawful Marginal
Core Instinct	One more optimization
Blind Spot	The line that went up while the other line went down
Passive Trait	Green Arrow
Party Role	Cost tuner
Primary Damage	Engineering attention spent on rounding errors
Weakness	“What did the savings buy?”
Signature Line	“We could shave another four percent.”

The Ghost in the Ledger

slopcodex.com/bestiary/ghost-in-the-ledger

A FinOps analyst presents a ledger while a hidden spectral assistant writes the analysis behind them.

The Ghost in the Ledger produces the best forecast the finance team has ever seen. It arrives on time, it is beautifully formatted, it catches anomalies nobody else caught, and nobody can explain how. When the Ghost goes on vacation, the forecast stops. When someone opens the spreadsheet, there is one cell that says `=AI(...)` and a link to a personal account.

The Ghost is not cheating. The Ghost found a tool that works and did what everyone has been told to do with AI, which is use it. The problem is that the organization now has a critical financial process with a bus factor of one, and the bus is a Google Sheet. The output cannot be reproduced, reviewed, or handed off. Nobody knows what data the model saw, what it was asked, or which of its numbers a human checked. The organization believes it has a stronger FinOps function. It has one person and a prompt.

The AI version is stranger than the old “indispensable analyst” problem because the method is genuinely invisible. There is no macro to inspect. There is a conversation that happened in a browser tab, and the tab is closed.

Recognition Signals

- A sudden productivity jump has no explanation and no process change.
- Reports cannot be reproduced by another analyst.
- The organization rewards the output but never records the method.
- A model has access to financial data through an account nobody in security has heard of.

Counter-Moves

Require a production note. Inputs, tool, model, checks performed, reviewer, known gaps. Half a page. If the method cannot be written down, the work is not finished.

Turn the private tool into a team tool. Pair people on important reports and rotate ownership. The goal is keeping the good work when the Ghost changes jobs, not catching anyone.

Character Sheet: Ghost in the Ledger

Trait	Notes
Category	FinOps
Archetype	Ghost in the Ledger
Alignment	Neutral Undocumented
Core Instinct	Get the number right, privately
Blind Spot	A method nobody can see is a dependency nobody can manage
Passive Trait	Bus Factor of One
Party Role	Star analyst
Primary Damage	Unreproducible forecast; unreviewed data access
Weakness	“Walk me through how this was produced.”
Signature Line	“I have a process.”

The Dashboard Necromancer

slopcodex.com/bestiary/dashboard-necromancer

A hooded figure raises a glowing dashboard from a cauldron of incomplete data, projecting a confident trend line into darkness.

The Dashboard Necromancer can raise a chart that ends any argument. In the expansion meeting, the Necromancer summons cost-per-user at pilot scale, and it is small, and the room relaxes. In the cost-cutting meeting, the Necromancer summons total spend for the same tool, and it is large, and the room panics. Both charts are accurate. Neither answers the question the room needed answered, which was what this costs at the scale we are about to commit to.

The Necromancer's dashboard shows token spend, so the organization assumes it shows AI economics. It omits retries, cache behavior, review labor, latency, and value. Unknown costs are treated as zero, which is the only accounting method in which the unknown is free. And the line is smooth. AI workloads do not have smooth lines. They have cliffs: a model release, a longer context window, a team that discovered the tool, an agent loop that discovered itself. The Necromancer's chart draws a gentle slope through all of it.

The Necromancer is often not trying to deceive anyone. The dashboard was built for the question someone asked six months ago. It has simply been answering that question ever since, in rooms that have moved on to different questions.

Recognition Signals

- Spend is visible; value is not.
- The graph is smooth through a workload that has step changes.
- Unknown costs appear as zero.
- The dashboard answers "what happened?" but never "what should we do?"

Counter-Moves

Add a "what we do not know" panel. Retries, review time, cache behavior, and unattributed usage go on the dashboard as named gaps. A dashboard that names its blind spots is more useful than a precise one that hides them.

Tie every cost view to a workload and an outcome. Cost per resolved ticket, per reviewed document, per deployed change. Use normalized telemetry where you can, including the FOCUS extensions being built for AI cost data. A dashboard should help a team make a decision, not help a meeting feel controlled.

Character Sheet: Dashboard Necromancer

Trait	Notes
Category	FinOps
Archetype	Dashboard Necromancer
Alignment	Chaotic Visualized
Core Instinct	Summon the chart the room is ready to believe
Blind Spot	The measurement is not the economics
Passive Trait	Smooth Line
Party Role	Meeting closer
Primary Damage	Confident decisions on incomplete numbers
Weakness	"What is not on this chart?"
Signature Line	"As you can see from the trend…"

Artifacts

FinOps artifacts are the documents these characters bring into the room. Each one is accurate. Each one answers a different question than the one being asked.

The Forecast of Comfortable Linearity

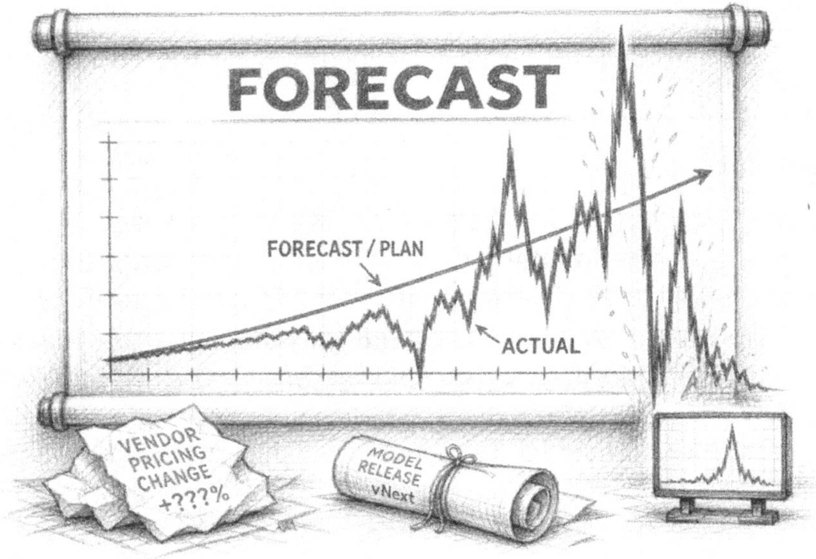

A smooth forecast line is overtaken by jagged actual demand spikes that make the linear projection obviously wrong.

Stats: Budget Approval +5, Executive Calm +4, Cliff Awareness −5, Assumption Visibility −4

Wielded by: The Dashboard Necromancer

The Forecast draws last quarter's spend into next quarter with a ruler. It looks like planning. It is extrapolation with a font. AI workloads do not grow along a ruler; a model release, an expanded context window, a successful internal demo, or an agent loop can change the slope in a week, and the Forecast has no place to put a week.

Replace the one line with four: pilot, expected adoption, successful adoption, and rollback. Put the assumptions next to the numbers. A forecast that names its cliffs is more useful than a precise forecast that hides them.

The Ledger of Justified Enormity

A massive capital proposal document, open to a page of large numbers and curated evidence, with the unanswered questions barely visible in the margins.

Stats: Line-Item Defensibility +5, Program Continuity +4, Total Defensibility −5, Stopping Condition −5

Wielded by: The CapEx Knight

The Ledger turns a large AI program into a list of reasons it must continue. Every line is defensible. The total is not, because nobody connected the spend to a result, and a list of individually reasonable expenses is how organizations end up funding things nobody chose.

Replace it with a decision ledger: workload, owner, cost to serve, expected value, evidence so far, next review date, and the condition that would stop the work. That last column is the one the Ledger of Justified Enormity never has.

The Unit Cost Abacus

A compact cost-tracking abacus sits in the foreground, while a dragon-sized business problem remains visible and unaddressed in the background.

Stats: Token Precision +5, Tuning Enablement +3, Business Relevance −4, Value Visibility −5

Wielded by: The Efficiency Evangelist

The Abacus counts tokens to the fourth decimal place and cannot tell you whether the system is worth running. Token cost is a fine atomic measure, but the business unit is a resolved ticket, a reviewed document, a deployed change, or a completed customer interaction, and none of those appear on the Abacus.

Keep both views. Track tokens so the system can be tuned. Track cost per completed unit so the organization can decide whether to keep tuning it or turn it off.

The Pilot That Proved It

A framed certificate held up confidently while a crowd of thousands approaches from the background and concurrency meters spin up around the frame.

Stats: Rollout Momentum +5, Stakeholder Enthusiasm +5, Production Representativeness −5, Cost Predictiveness −4

Wielded by: The Avalanche Skeptic

The Pilot is ten users, a friendly dataset, a short prompt, and one of the builders sitting nearby to fix anything that breaks. It worked. It was cheap. It is now being presented as proof that four thousand users with hostile data, a long prompt, and no builder nearby will also be cheap.

A real pilot records the conditions that made it work and states what it did not test. That makes the next decision better without pretending the answer is already known.

Spells

FinOps spells move the cost conversation somewhere it cannot be found. Each has a counterspell, and each counterspell is a question you can ask before the next expansion.

The Innovation Ward

A project manager tosses an AI cost ownership ticket into a Later bucket while a teammate asks how to pay for it this year.

Casting time: Any meeting where the word "innovation" appears before the word "budget." Components: a demo, a deadline, and the phrase "let's not slow this down."

The caster moves every hard question to later: price, ownership, data access, quality, the cost of success. Later is a comfortable place. Nothing ever has to be decided there. Meanwhile adoption continues, and by the time later arrives the tool has a constituency.

Counterspell: "Can we have a one-page estimate before the next expansion?" It can be wrong. It cannot be absent.

The Budget Teleport

One AI workload splits chargeback fragments across departments so everyone and no one owns the full cost.

Casting time: Any allocation meeting. Components: three cost centers, one workload, and a chart of accounts nobody has updated for AI.

The caster distributes a single workload across departments until nobody can see its full cost. The model bill is on the platform team. The vector database is on data engineering. The human review is on customer support. Each department's number is fine. The workload's number does not exist.

Counterspell: "Follow the workload." Allocate every cost that makes the outcome possible, not just the invoice that is easiest to assign.

The Methodology Mist

A presenter says not to worry about the details while mist hides a tangled machinery layer of prompts, formulas, scripts, and model outputs.

Casting time: Any report review. Components: a polished forecast, a confident presenter, and no appendix.

The caster produces an impressive analysis and lets the process stay invisible. The output looks rigorous because nobody can see how it was made, and nobody asks because the number is what they hoped for.

Counterspell: "What produced this?" Inputs, model, checks, reviewer, uncertainty. Half a page is enough to let someone else challenge or repeat the work.

A Practical Tokenomics Loop

The positive version of this chapter fits on an index card.

1. **Name the workload** and the unit of completed work.
2. **Measure the request:** input, output, reasoning, and cached tokens; retries; tool calls; model route.
3. **Build the full cost:** infrastructure, software, data, engineering, and human review, not just the token line.

4. **Connect cost to value:** completion, quality, time saved, revenue, or risk avoided.
5. **Pick the operating point** on cost to serve and quality, not token count alone.
6. **Review at the cliff:** recalculate when adoption, context, model, autonomy, or service expectations change.

The meter is more complicated than it used to be. The purpose is the same: give people enough information to make a decision while the decision is still reversible.

Closing

Somewhere in your organization right now, a pilot is succeeding. Somebody loves it. Somebody has added it to a workflow. Somebody has turned on the reasoning model because the answers got better. And somebody in finance is going to notice on a Thursday afternoon.

The question worth asking before Thursday is not "how do we eliminate AI spend?" It is "what work are we buying, what does it cost to serve, and what result earns the cost?" That question leaves room for experiments, rewards the systems that work, and makes failure visible before it becomes infrastructure.

CHAPTER 4

Architect NPCs and Anti-Patterns

Architects are supposed to help the organization think clearly before it commits. That is the healthy version of the role: someone who can step back from the immediate implementation, notice the shape of the problem, ask what must be true for the design to work, and help the team decide whether the system can actually be built, operated, and changed.

Good architects translate ambiguity into choices. They know when a problem is really about data flow, when it is about ownership, when it is about latency, and when the team is trying to solve a product problem with an infrastructure diagram because the diagram is less emotionally complicated than talking to product managers. In the AI era that role matters more, not less. A Large Language Model (LLM) can generate plausible plans all day, but someone still has to decide whether the plan describes a system the organization can operate, explain, govern, and repair. A good architect is the difference between "We vibe coded this and we're not sure how it works" and "Generative AI helped build this, and we understand the design."

The trouble starts when architectural authority detaches from current technical reality. AI has made that detachment easier to spot because it is now so easy to generate a disconnected mess that still sounds like an architecture. The person whose instincts were excellent in 2006 may still have excellent instincts, but the instincts need contact with the present. The person who built a career on being better than the tools may be right to distrust hype, but not if distrust becomes a permanent refusal to notice what the tools can do.

There is also a career story underneath this role. An architect is usually not a new developer's first job. Many architects got there after years of programming, operating systems, reviewing designs, and learning which shortcuts become incidents later. That experience is real. But in a lot of organizations the role has drifted toward telling programmers what to build while staying several steps away from the implementation. Generative AI is putting pressure on that arrangement. Claude Code, Codex, Cursor, and similar agents can inspect a repository, propose a plan, edit files, run tests, use tools, and revise the result. They do not need an architect to dictate every class, interface, or design pattern before a programmer is allowed to begin.

They still need guidance. Someone has to define the goal, identify the constraints, choose what may be delegated, review what came back, and understand the system well enough to reject a confident mistake. The emerging job is less "tell programmers how to code" and more "design the conditions in which humans and agents can produce software safely." That is a real architectural contribution. The older version of the role—standing above implementation and issuing instructions from a whiteboard—does not fit a world where the implementation can arrive before the architecture meeting ends.

Baseline Architect Role

At their best, architects give teams a place to put complexity. They ask which decisions are reversible, which constraints are real, which assumptions have been tested, and which diagram exists mainly because everyone was tired and someone felt like drawing a box on a whiteboard. Architects are not there to "do architecture" so much as to help developers think about the problems that are bigger than the ticket.

In AI systems that job is harder because so much of the work arrives wearing the costume of "done." Ask the system for a website and, just like that, there is a website, and it looks amazing. A good architect knows where to look. "Okay, the React site showed up in five minutes and looks like it went to design school. Did anyone check the database schema? It's awful."

The healthy architect asks about the problem. What is the input? Who owns the output? What happens when the model is wrong? What does the human review? What is logged? What can be rolled back? What part of this is engineering, and what part is someone hoping an LLM will compensate for a product manager who is too busy vibe coding to write requirements?

Most architect anti-patterns appear when the architect stops doing that work and starts substituting authority for understanding. The first sign is a meeting where the architect talks more than anyone else and nobody asks a follow-up. The second is a design document that could have been written two years ago with only the product name changed. The third is an architect who is always available for the whiteboard session and never available for the incident review. The distance between the diagram and the production system is where these Non-player Characters (NPCs) live.

The Architect Cast

The Architect cast has three figures. The **Agent Whisperer** turns demo-shaped possibility into internal certainty before anyone has proved the system works. The **Legacy Laureate** built something great somewhere else, long ago, and brings every current discussion back to it. The **Last Stand Architect** treats AI-generated architecture as an invasion to be resisted rather than a capability to be evaluated.

None of them start from a bad instinct, which is what makes them tricky. Fluency, experience, and standards are all real strengths. Each becomes a problem when it stops paying attention to the decision in front of it.

The Agent Whisperer

slopcodex.com/bestiary/agent-whisperer

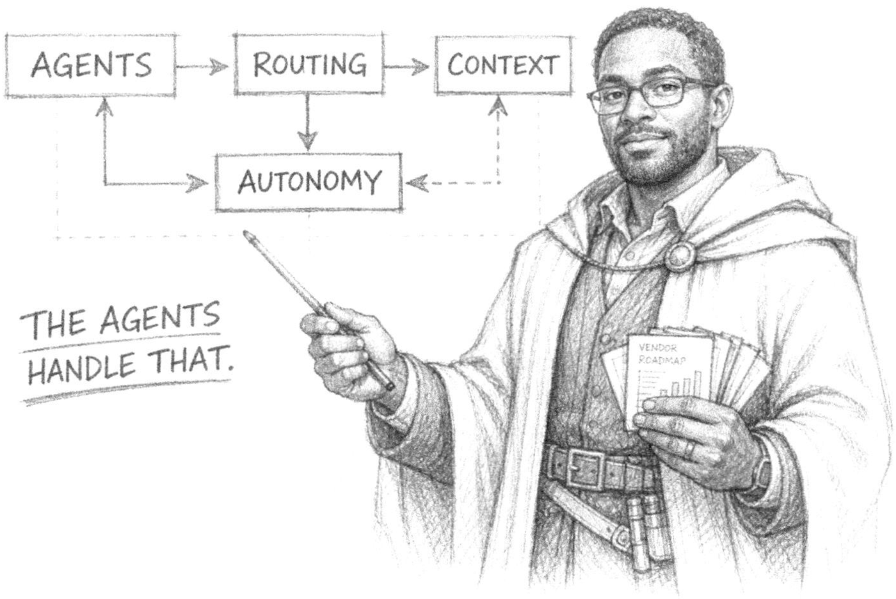

An architect presents an unproven agent orchestration diagram as if the future system already works.

The Agent Whisperer can explain the agentic AI terrain with enough fluency that everyone else in the room feels slightly behind. At their best, they are extremely useful. They can stop an organization from adopting too slowly out of fear, and from adopting too naively out of excitement.

The trouble starts when fluency turns into confidence on its own. The Whisperer's signature move is speaking about the near future in the present tense. "The agents handle that." "The system routes the work." "The model figures out the context." Each sentence makes the future sound already implemented, and the organization starts designing governance, staffing, and budget around a system that has been described more completely than it has been proven.

Then the description starts traveling. Suddenly a vice president is talking about how incredible it will be when the whole company automates planning with "Gas City" and replaces Jira with Beads, because the issue tracker is apparently the thing holding back civilization. A prototype becomes a roadmap. A roadmap becomes a staffing model. A staffing model becomes a moral test of whether you are brave enough to delete the humans from the workflow.

The Whisperer can start to sound insane because the job title has become a prophecy. They talk about agent fleet managers, context engineers, prompt operations directors, autonomous product teams, and other roles that may be useful descriptions someday but do not yet describe a staffed, budgeted, accountable job. They speak about a world that has not been achieved yet as if it were an org chart waiting to be printed. The problem is not imagination. The problem is skipping the awkward middle: the current tools, the current failure rate, the current permissions, the current review queue, and the current person who gets paged when the agent does something expensive or dangerous.

Modern agentic programming makes the distinction sharper. Agents can plan, edit, run tests, call tools, and work for hours or days, but the human role has not vanished. It has moved toward decomposition, orchestration, evaluation, and verification. A future-tense job title is not evidence that those responsibilities have been solved. It is a prompt for an experiment.

The Whisperer is not usually lying. Their explanation has simply become a substitute for verification. The room stops asking "what have we actually tested?" because the story of what is coming sounds so coherent that it feels like evidence.

Recognition Signals

- The phrase "agents will handle that" appears before anyone has defined the failure mode.
- The architecture diagram includes autonomous handoffs that have not been tested with real users, real data, or real exception paths.
- Vendor roadmap language comes back into the organization sounding like internal engineering judgment.
- Doubt becomes socially expensive because the Whisperer seems to know something everyone else does not.
- The future tense quietly disappears from the conversation.
- "No one looks at code any more," becomes a common refrain whenever anyone expresses doubt.

Counter-Moves

Separate fluency from proof. Treat the Whisperer's explanation as useful orientation, not as evidence that the system works. Ask what has been tested, under what conditions, with what failure cases, and by whom.

Keep the tense honest. If the capability is future, say future. If it works in a demo, say demo. If it works in production, say production. The tense of the sentence is an architectural control.

Require a rollback story. Any agentic architecture that cannot explain what happens when the agent is wrong is not ready to be treated as architecture. It is still a proposal.

Watch the wallet. If the Agent Whisperer gets too much influence without cost checks, the organization can start burning tokens faster than anyone thought possible. Every autonomous handoff, retry loop, evaluation pass, and "just let the model figure it out" decision has a meter attached.

Ask for the present-tense job. When a new role appears in the story, name the work it performs today, the system it owns, the evidence that the work is needed, and the decision rights attached to it. If nobody can answer, keep the title in the notebook instead of the org chart.

Character Sheet: Agent Whisperer

Trait	Notes
Category	Architect
Archetype	Agent Whisperer
Alignment	Lawful Speculative
Core Instinct	Translate the agentic future into organizational language
Blind Spot	Fluency can outrun proof
Passive Trait	Present-Tense Roadmap
Party Role	Technical credibility engine
Primary Damage	Premature certainty
Weakness	"What have we actually tested?"
Signature Line	"The agents can handle that."

The Legacy Laureate

slopcodex.com/bestiary/legacy-laureate

An accomplished architect presents a glowing former-platform blueprint while the current AI diagram waits ignored.

The Legacy Laureate once worked on something genuinely impressive and has never stopped architecting from the afterglow. The achievement was real. The Laureate is not inventing the past. They are trapped in it.

You will meet this person in a discussion about the current AI architecture, and within ten minutes the meeting will have traveled to a former employer, a former platform, or a former standard that apparently solved all of this twenty years ago. The team is trying to decide how to evaluate retrieval quality in an LLM-backed workflow. The Laureate is explaining how a previous company handled enterprise service bus governance in 2004. There may be a connection. There is usually less of one than the story implies.

The damage is the meeting tax. Every interaction with the Laureate carries a silent 30 to 40 percent surcharge while the room politely listens to the story from the other place. Everyone knows the tax exists. Nobody wants to be rude enough to name it. And the tax is especially expensive in generative AI conversations because the present really is different: probabilistic output, prompt-sensitive behavior, model drift, and vendor-controlled capability changes all break the old reference points. The Laureate keeps unrolling a map of an ancient city. The team is not in that city. The Laureate may still know how the old city was built, but that does not mean they know where the new roads, traffic, and power grid are. The Laureate may still know how the old city was built, but that does not mean they know where the new roads, traffic, and power grid are.

Recognition Signals

- The meeting title might as well be "Please Tell Me More About How Wonderful The Work Was You Did 20 Years Ago."
- Current AI questions are repeatedly translated into the architecture politics of a former employer.
- The story begins with "when we did this at..." and ends after the decision window has quietly closed.
- The Laureate treats old success as portable authority, even when the current system has different economics, failure modes, and user expectations.
- Other senior people schedule pre-meetings to get the real work done before the story tax begins when the Laureate says, "Hey this reminds me of..."
- The Laureate starts recruiting a small court of former colleagues from the other company, importing the old language and increasing the story tax.

Counter-Moves

Extract the principle, then return to the present. "What is the lesson from that system that applies here?" is a respectful question. It lets the experience matter without letting the meeting become a museum tour.

Time-box the analogy on an agenda. Give the past a short, explicit window. If the story cannot produce a present-tense decision, it is not architecture input. It is color commentary. "Does anyone have any experience that might be helpful? I've built 5 minutes into the schedule for that."

Name the changed condition. Ask what is different in the AI version: probabilistic output, model ownership, data sensitivity, feedback loops, governance, cost shape, or human review. The Laureate can often contribute once the comparison is forced to update.

Test portability instead of importing prestige. Ask which parts of the former success depended on the old company's data, distribution, platform, talent density, incentives, and scale. A proven leader may bring useful principles and a trusted network. They may also bring a playbook that worked because the old organization supplied half the solution. Research on star knowledge workers found that performance often depends on firm-specific resources and that stars can lose performance after moving.[12] Research on CEO succession likewise finds that prior experience is no guarantee of performance in a new context.[13] The question is not whether the Laureate was brilliant. The question is which parts of that brilliance survive the move.

Invoke the non-disclosure agreement. A gentle reminder that former employers had internal processes, confidential constraints, and actual non-disclosure agreements can keep the room from treating someone else's architecture history as reusable company property. The lesson may travel. The proprietary details should not.

Character Sheet: Legacy Laureate

Trait	Notes
Category	Architect
Archetype	Legacy Laureate
Alignment	Lawful Remembered
Core Instinct	Reuse the wisdom of the system that made them important
Blind Spot	The present problem is not their greatest past success
Passive Trait	Meeting Tax
Party Role	Historical authority source
Primary Damage	Decision drag
Weakness	"What changed since then?"
Signature Line	"At my previous company…"

[12] Boris Groysberg, Lex Sant, and Robin Abrahams, MIT Sloan Management Review, "When 'Stars' Migrate, Do They Still Perform Like Stars?", 2008. The research describes how star performance can depend on firm-specific resources and may not transfer intact when the individual changes organizations.

[13] Claudius A. Hildebrand, Cathy Anterasian, and Jordan L. Brugg, Spencer Stuart, "Predicting CEO Success: When Potential Outperforms Experience". Their analysis of 855 S&P 500 CEOs found no premium for prior CEO experience and warns that a proven playbook can limit new thinking when applied too rigidly in a new context.

The Last Stand Architect

slopcodex.com/bestiary/last-stand-architect

A senior architect blocks an AI-generated design with a drafting shield instead of evaluating it.

The Last Stand Architect refuses to admit that AI can do architecture or programming in any meaningful sense. Their identity was built through code, judgment, taste, and hard-won credibility. They got where they are by being better than the tools around them. Now a tool has arrived that generates plausible code, plausible diagrams, and plausible tradeoff analyses on demand, and the Last Stand Architect experiences it as an invasion.

This character is often near the end of a long engineering career. They may have spent decades moving from programming into design reviews, standards, governance, and architecture, until their full-time job became telling other programmers what to do. That path produced valuable judgment, but it also created a role that assumes implementation is downstream of architectural instruction. Agentic coding breaks that sequence. Claude Code, Codex, and Cursor can take a requirement, inspect the repository, make a plan, change the code, run tests, and return a diff before the traditional architecture lecture has finished. The tools do not eliminate the need for architectural judgment. They reduce the need for someone to narrate every implementation step to another human.

The replacement work is harder and less ceremonial: define boundaries, set acceptance tests, expose the important context, decide what the agent may change, review the result, and keep enough understanding to operate what was built. An architect who learns that work can remain central. An architect who insists that the old distance from code is the job is defending a disappearing arrangement, not defending engineering.

The Last Stand Architect is often arguing with developers who have already changed their workflow. Those developers may not be reading every line of generated code anymore. They may be asking an agent to handle tactical implementation, run the tests, explain the diff, and return when something fails. That does not automatically mean they are careless. It means the volume of generated code has made line-by-line human inspection a contested strategy rather than an unquestioned duty.

The disagreement is not really about whether AI-generated code should be trusted. It is about what developers are learning as the tools improve: inspection of every line may not be necessary for every change. They are learning to spend attention on behavior, boundaries, tests, security, data access, dependencies, and blast radius, while delegating more tactical implementation detail to the tool. The Last Stand Architect may believe they are defending engineering discipline. The developers may be wondering whether the architect understands what has changed—and whether the architect's own demonstrated capabilities have kept pace with the job.

That last question is uncomfortable without being ageist. This is not about whether someone is old. It is about whether the skills that earned a promotion still match the work the organization now needs. Architecture has sometimes become a reward for having been excellent at an earlier kind of engineering: write the code, master the patterns, advise the teams, and gradually move farther from the keyboard. The title can survive after the hands-on capability, context, and curiosity that justified it have expired. An architect can be experienced and still be out of date. Those are not opposites.

This pattern has a noble version. Someone should be skeptical. Someone should ask whether the generated design is coherent, whether the code can be maintained, and whether the organization is confusing speed with quality. The anti-pattern appears when skepticism hardens into refusal.

You can hear the refusal in absolutes. "AI cannot design systems." "This is autocomplete with a marketing budget." "Anyone relying on this does not understand engineering." Softened, some of those sentences contain a useful warning. The Last Stand Architect does not soften them, because the sentence is doing identity work.

The cost is that the team loses a senior person's judgment exactly where it is needed. Instead of helping define where AI is useful, where it is dangerous, and what review would make it safer, the Last Stand Architect stands outside the adoption curve and fires arrows at it. The arrows sometimes hit real problems. They also make everyone stop inviting the archer to planning meetings.

Sidebar: The Review Debate Is Not Hypothetical

There used to be an easy answer to the question of generated code: read it. Treat the model like a junior developer. Inspect every line, understand every branch, and do not merge anything you cannot explain. That is still the right standard for sensitive code, unfamiliar dependencies, authentication, payments, data handling, and changes whose failure would be expensive.

But the volume and shape of generated software are changing the argument. Sonar's 2026 State of Code Developer Survey reports that developers say 42 percent of the code they commit is already AI-generated or AI-assisted, and that 72 percent of developers who have tried AI coding tools use them every day.[14] The same report says AI is being used not only for prototypes but for 73 percent of customer-facing applications and 58 percent of mission-critical services. Its headline finding is blunt:

> *"96% of developers don't fully trust that AI-generated code is functionally correct."*

That combination matters. Developers are using AI constantly while remaining aware that the output is not automatically correct. Some teams are responding by reviewing the change at the level of behavior, tests, security controls, architecture, and blast radius instead of reading every generated line with equal attention. Others are using agent loops, automated tests, static analysis, AI review, staged rollouts, and production telemetry as part of the verification system. Neither approach is a license to stop understanding the

[14]Sonar, "2026 State of Code Developer Survey report", based on 1,149 professional developers surveyed in October 2025. The report gives the 42 percent AI-assisted/generated figure, the 72 percent daily-use figure, the customer-facing and mission-critical adoption figures, and the quoted 96 percent trust finding.

software. It is a response to the fact that an agent can produce more code in an afternoon than a human can inspect line by line in the same afternoon.

The DORA 2025 report captures the organizational version of the problem: "AI doesn't fix a team; it amplifies what's already there."[15] A team with strong tests, clear ownership, fast feedback, and disciplined review can delegate more tactical work safely. A team without those controls can generate a large, polished pile of mistakes. The Last Stand Architect is right that generated code needs verification. The team is right that verification cannot mean pretending the old volume of manual inspection still scales unchanged.

The useful argument is therefore not "read every line" versus "read nothing." It is: what evidence is required before this change is trusted, which parts demand human understanding, and which checks can be automated or delegated? When the Last Stand Architect refuses that question, developers may reasonably conclude that the architect is defending a ritual rather than helping them build a safer system.

Recognition Signals

- AI capability claims are rejected before the specific workflow is discussed.
- The architect rejects generated code because a model produced it, not because anyone has found a real problem in the code.
- Every successful AI-assisted result is described as trivial, lucky, or not "real engineering."
- The team stops bringing AI questions to the architect because the answer is known in advance.
- The architect's skepticism becomes less useful as the team needs more concrete review standards.
- If a Legacy Laureate shows up, the combination of the two can result in uninterruptible meeting paralysis.

Counter-Moves

Move from yes/no to boundary-setting. Do not ask whether AI can do architecture. Ask which parts of architectural work can be assisted, which must remain human-owned, and what review standard applies to each. Run experiments and provide evidence before asking. The useful question is not whether

[15]Nathen Harvey and Derek DeBellis, "Announcing the 2025 DORA Report: State of AI-Assisted Software Development", Google Cloud. The report is based on survey responses from nearly 5,000 technology professionals and uses the phrase "AI doesn't fix a team; it amplifies what's already there."

an agent can write the code. It is whether the team can explain, test, secure, operate, and change the result.

Make them responsible for the rubric. The Last Stand Architect's skepticism becomes useful when it turns into criteria: what makes generated code acceptable, what makes an AI-generated design unsafe, what evidence would change their mind.

Protect the identity while changing the work. The point is not to humiliate the person who built real expertise. The point is to redirect that expertise toward evaluating AI output instead of denying that the output matters.

Character Sheet: Last Stand Architect

Trait	Notes
Category	Architect
Archetype	Last Stand Architect
Alignment	Lawful Defensive
Core Instinct	Defend human architecture against generated plausibility
Blind Spot	Refusal is not the same as judgment
Passive Trait	Valiant Gatekeeping
Party Role	Skeptical standard-bearer
Primary Damage	Lost senior judgment
Weakness	"What evidence would change your mind?"
Signature Line	"AI cannot do real architecture."

How to Spot Architect Dynamics

The Legacy Laureate has a research-backed failure mode. Carnegie Mellon's Software Engineering Institute describes a "wraparound" pattern in which an architect who successfully sustained a legacy system is selected to design its replacement, even though their current technology and development practices may be out of sync with the team. The old success is real. The mismatch is real too.[16]

[16] John Klein, Carnegie Mellon Software Engineering Institute, "Three Roles and Three Failure Patterns of Software Architects", 2016. Klein calls the pattern "wraparound" and warns that an architect who sustained a legacy system may be out of sync with the technologies, practices, and tools used by the team building its replacement.

The common thread is the gap between authority and evidence. The Whisperer has authority without testing. The Laureate has authority without currency. The Last Stand has authority without engagement. When an architect's conclusions arrive faster than their questions, when their references point backward more often than forward, or when their diagrams describe a world the team does not live in yet, one of these patterns is forming.

The current evidence points to a change in the work, not the disappearance of architecture. Martin Fowler describes agentic programming as a shift in which humans oversee LLM agents that generate code while remaining responsible for what the software does and how it works.[17] Anthropic's 2026 agentic coding report describes the human role moving toward system design, agent coordination, quality evaluation, and problem decomposition, with longer-running agents producing whole systems over hours or days.[18] Research on future software-profession skills makes the same warning from another direction: verification and validation become more important as agents take on implementation, because teams can accumulate cognitive debt when people lose the intent and rationale behind machine-generated systems.[19] That is the modern architect's opening. Not more diagrams. Better constraints, better tests, better questions, and enough technical contact with the system to know when the agent is confidently wrong.

---

[17]Martin Fowler, "Agentic Programming", May 21, 2026. Fowler describes developers prompting LLMs to generate code, then reviewing the results while remaining responsible for the software.

[18]Anthropic, "2026 Agentic Coding Trends Report". The report describes a shift from implementer to orchestrator and the rise of long-running agents.

[19]S. Teki et al., "Skills for the future software profession: beyond agentic AI!", arXiv:2606.21894v2, 2026. The paper discusses verification and validation, and the risk of cognitive debt when developers lose understanding of AI-maintained software.

Artifacts

Architect artifacts are the objects they carry into meetings: stories, frameworks, and diagrams that look useful because they resemble leadership. Generative AI makes them easier to produce and easier to polish.

The Amulet of Past Glory

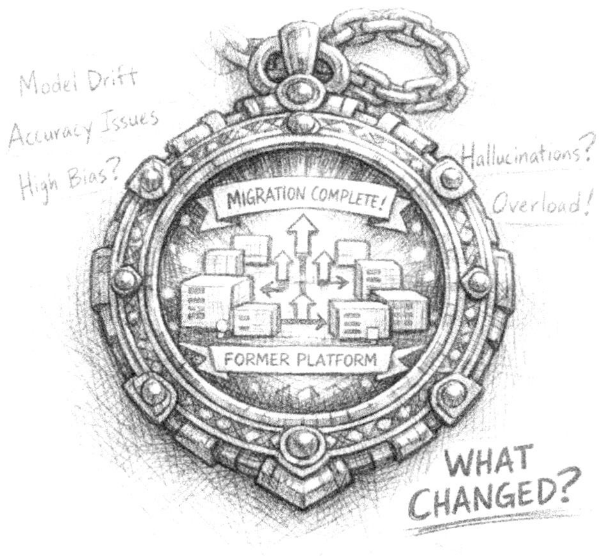

A secular trophy amulet glows with a former platform success while current AI review notes fade behind it.

Stats: Narrative Authority +5, Room Deference +4, Present-Tense Relevance −4, Meeting Velocity −5

Wielded by: The Legacy Laureate

The Amulet gives every current AI problem a former employer, a former platform, and a story that begins before half the team had a LinkedIn profile. The team asks how to handle prompt sensitivity in a retrieval-augmented workflow. The Laureate answers with a story about schema versioning in a service-oriented architecture from 2008. The team nods, takes the versioning lesson, and leaves without an answer to the question they asked.

I have held the Amulet. The next time you catch yourself saying "when I was at my previous company," try stopping after the principle and asking: "Does this still apply here? What has changed?"

Spells

Architect spells make AI architecture feel finished before the hard work has happened. They are not only cast by people with "architect" in their title. Product leaders, staff engineers, consultants, and whoever owns the most convincing generated diagram can all pick them up. The better architect does not cast bigger spells. They cast fewer, and they are painfully specific about when and why.

The Box-and-Arrow Blizzard

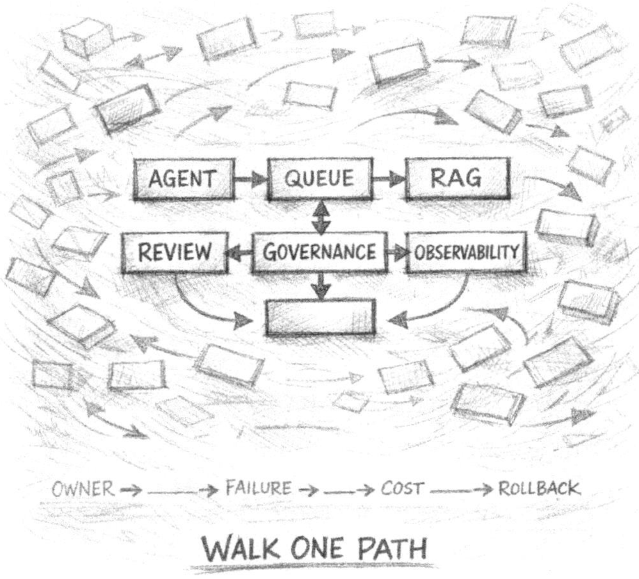

A storm of confident architecture boxes and arrows hides the untested real path through an AI system.

Casting time: One prompt, one blank diagramming canvas, and a meeting where everyone wants the system to make sense already.

The caster conjures an enormous, fully formed AI system diagram out of thin air, often with help from the same tools the team is supposed to be evaluating. Every box is labeled. Every arrow travels with the confidence of a line that has never encountered production traffic, prompt drift, or a user doing something weird. The diagram looks complete, which is the trick. People stop asking what has been validated because the artifact looks like the answer.

There is a particular version that deserves attention: the diagram that includes an "Evaluation Framework" box. The box has an arrow going in and an arrow going out. It does not have a definition of what it evaluates, how it evaluates, who reviews the results, or what metric would cause the team to change the model. The box is a placeholder for work that has not been done, and the Blizzard has made the placeholder look like the work.

Counterspell: Pick one path through the diagram and walk it with real input, a real owner, a model failure, a cost estimate, and the rollback story. If the path cannot survive that walk, the diagram is not architecture yet.

The Decoupling Fog Machine

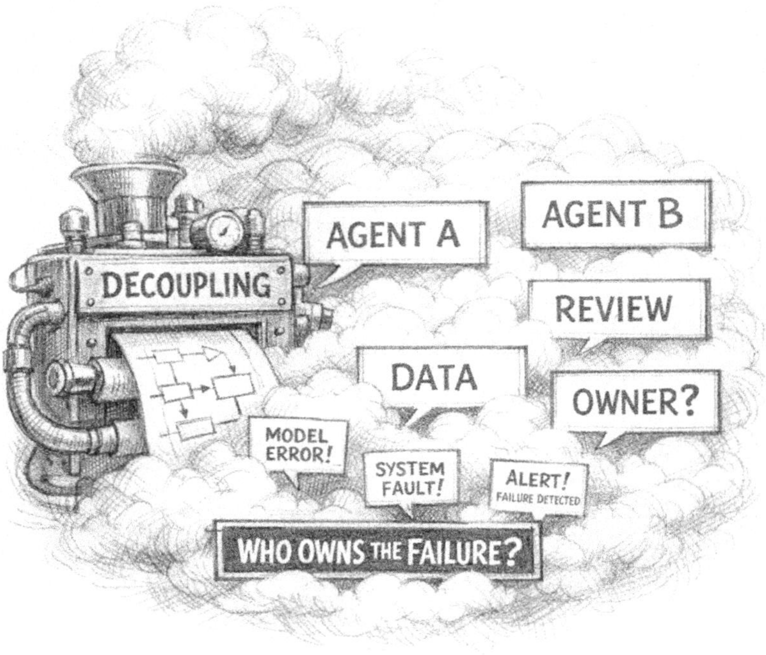

A decoupling fog machine makes an AI workflow diagram cleaner while pager alerts lose their owner.

Casting time: One architecture review where "clean boundaries" sounds more measurable than ownership.

The caster restructures the AI system for decoupling, and the paper design immediately improves. Responsibilities move into cleaner boxes. Agents get narrower jobs. Interfaces become more elegant. The diagram relaxes. Unfortunately, the pager does not.

This is the safest-looking spell. It uses words architects are supposed to like: separation, modularity, abstraction, boundary. Everything is cleaner on paper, but ownership becomes fuzzy, on-call boundaries blur, and failures cross invisible lines. When a generated action is wrong, three teams are involved and none of them are sure they are the team.

Counterspell: Put an owner, a pager, and a model-failure example on every boundary. If an agent, component, or generated action can fail in production, someone has to know whether they are responsible before the alert fires.

Closing

"We did this in 2019 and it worked" is not a design document. It is a memoir. The best architects are not the people with the most stories, the strongest opinions, or the most fluent agent vocabulary. They are the people who make the next decision clearer than it was before they entered the room.

CHAPTER 5

Vendor NPCs and Anti-Patterns

Software vendors have always shaped engineering culture. AI vendors just do it with more tempo, more theater, and a much stronger instinct for turning roadmap uncertainty into a performance of destiny.

That does not make vendors uniquely evil. It makes them vendors. Their job is to create preference, urgency, and a path from interest to contract. Most organizations learn about new capabilities through vendors, conference keynotes, benchmark reports, and partner briefings, and some of that is how genuinely good tools spread. The trouble begins when vendor language stops being external input and becomes internal self-understanding. The market is changing fast enough that buyers feel status anxiety in real time. Nobody wants to be the executive who missed the platform shift. Nobody wants to admit that half the urgency in the room came from a podcast or a graph with no denominator.

In AI, the cast is obvious. OpenAI is a vendor. Anthropic is a vendor. xAI is a vendor. NVIDIA is a vendor, even when it arrives wearing the ceremonial robes of infrastructure. They are all selling different pieces of a related story: the future is arriving now, it is arriving at unprecedented speed, and they are among the few organizations able to give you access to it. Sometimes that story is true. It is still a sales story. Vendor influence in this era feels less like weather and more like a conman who has learned to bring charts. You do not merely buy a product. You buy urgency, identity, a relationship, and a fear that the door will close if you ask for another week.

None of this means you should ignore vendors. You should know when you are being informed, when you are being marketed to, and when your organization has quietly started mistaking AI as a tool for AI as a trophy.

Baseline Vendor Relationship

A healthy vendor relationship is a learning relationship. You learn from their experience across hundreds of customers; they learn from your use cases. It works when the buyer has a clear problem and the vendor has a specific solution. It starts to break when the conversation drifts from "can this solve our problem?" to "what does the market say we should be doing?" The first question is answerable. The second is a conference talk dressed as strategy.

A healthy relationship also has an exit plan. Not because the vendor is expected to fail, but because the organizations that manage vendors best treat every relationship as a capability they might one day need to replace. That sounds pessimistic. It is the discipline that keeps the pricing honest.

The buyer also needs to remember what the relationship is for. Vendor representatives are paid to create and close opportunities. They can be generous, funny, technically fluent, and genuinely helpful. They can also be doing their job while you are telling yourself that you have made a friend. The friendship may be real. The quota is real too. If the person disappears when procurement says no, the relationship has just provided its own footnote.

The trouble starts when the vendor layer begins narrating history on the company's behalf. Your competitors are already doing this. Agents are inevitable. The benchmark proves it. The roadmap gap is not a gap because a future release will close it. Once that language takes hold internally, the team is no longer evaluating a tool. It is role-playing inevitability, and everyone already knows what the answer is supposed to be.

The Vendor Cast

The archetypes below are not accusations that every salesperson is a fraud. They are reminders that the person across the table has incentives, a target, and a compensation plan. The charming one is still selling. The technical one is still selling. The one who skis at the same resort as your VP is definitely still selling.

The Vendor Bard

slopcodex.com/bestiary/vendor-bard

A charismatic bard in merchant's finery strums a lute made of roadmap slides, singing to an enraptured audience of executives.

The Vendor Bard is the charismatic singer of the new age. They sell capabilities, but mostly they sell status. Their gift is converting uncertainty into applause, and you hear them most clearly whenever a product is being described as a historical threshold rather than a bounded tool.

The Bard's signature move is turning market anxiety into identity. If you adopt the product, you are not buying software. You are joining the future. The Bard buffs optimism, debuffs skepticism, and leaves before the migration plan, the renewal negotiation, and the first ugly incident review. They arrive at the right moment: after a competitor announcement, during a period of executive anxiety, or just before a budget cycle where the initiative needs to sound transformational.

The Bard's real talent is making *not buying* feel like cowardice. "We should probably understand this better before committing" sounds prudent in a retrospective and feels like defeat in the room. The pressure is emotional rather than mechanical, and it works on people who know better.

Recognition Signals

- The conversation shifts from "can this solve our problem?" to "what are our competitors doing?" before anyone has described the problem.
- The pitch uses "paradigm," "generational," and "inevitable" more often than "latency," "error rate," and "migration cost."
- The vendor is noticeably less available after the contract is signed than before it.

Counter-Moves

Frame the evaluation around your problem, not the vendor's narrative. Before the demo, write down the three specific problems you need solved. After the demo, check whether any of them got addressed. If the pitch answered questions you did not ask and skipped the ones you did, the Bard is doing their job.

Ask "what does this not do well?" and watch the temperature of the answer. A vendor who can describe their product's limitations is worth listening to. A vendor who pivots to what competitors do not do is not answering your question.

Character Sheet: Vendor Bard

Trait	Notes
Category	Vendor
Archetype	Vendor Bard
Alignment	Chaotic Inspirational
Core Instinct	Convert market anxiety into social pressure
Blind Spot	Whether the product solves the buyer's specific problem
Passive Trait	FOMO Amplification
Party Role	Hype engine
Primary Damage	Evaluation replaced by enthusiasm
Weakness	"What does this not do well?"
Signature Line	"The companies that wait will be left behind."

The Friendly Familiar

A friendly vendor turns shared interests into trust while keeping a sales contract behind their back.

The Friendly Familiar does not begin with the product. They begin with you. Same hometown. Same university. Same industry association. Same favorite ski mountain. Same story about a difficult manager from twelve years ago. The details are harmless, which is why they work. A vendor who feels familiar gets mentally reclassified from interested party to trusted person, and trusted people get fewer hostile questions.

This is the Illusionist's softer trick: manufacture affinity, then let the buyer mistake affinity for aligned incentives. The Familiar may spend months helping with introductions, forwarding useful articles, remembering birthdays, and appearing at the right dinner. By the time the proposal arrives, nobody says, "The vendor is asking us to buy something." They say, "Our friend thinks this is the right move." The product has become a relationship with an invoice attached.

The conflict of interest can be creative rather than financial. A shared alma mater, hometown, board membership, family connection, conference circuit, or recreational habit may create pressure to be generous in the evaluation. No one has to take money. The relationship itself can make a tough question feel rude. That is enough to alter a decision.

Recognition Signals

- The vendor knows personal details that have little to do with the evaluation.
- Internal advocates describe the representative as a friend before they describe the product.
- A shared hometown, school, club, or hobby appears in the sales story as evidence of trustworthiness.
- The buyer starts protecting the vendor from procurement, security, or architecture questions.

Counter-Moves

Name the relationship without dramatizing it. Record personal, financial, advisory, and institutional connections that could reasonably affect the evaluation or appear to affect it. This is not an accusation. It is basic context.

Separate access from endorsement. A representative can earn a meeting, provide useful information, and still lose the decision. Keep the same evaluation rubric for the vendor you enjoy talking to and the vendor you find unbearable.

Ask who benefits if the relationship succeeds. The answer should include the customer, not only the account executive's commission, promotion, or next reference call.

The Purveyor of Doom

A vendor prophet sells an impending AI apocalypse with a contract in one hand and a price tag on the doomsday machine.

The Purveyor of Doom sells the product by announcing that the product is almost too dangerous to sell. The model is about to become autonomous. The safeguards are falling behind. Humans may lose control. The world has, according to the Purveyor's slide deck, approximately nine months left and one enterprise discount code.

This is mutually assured destruction as a sales technique. If you do not buy the dangerous system, your competitor will. If you do not give the vendor access to your data, somebody less responsible will give theirs to another vendor. If you do not support regulation, reckless competitors will win. If you do support regulation, the vendor is happy to help write the part that only a company with a hundred billion dollars of compute can afford to comply with.

The Purveyor may genuinely believe the warning. That is what makes the tactic useful. A warning can be sincere and still perform commercial work. The pitch has two preferred outcomes. First, government regulation should arrive quickly enough to raise the cost of entry for competitors, open models, and anyone without a government-relations department. Second, you should buy the next model from the Purveyor because it is the only model dangerous enough to require the regulation they just asked for and safe enough to sell you today.

Anthropic has publicly called for governments to gain authority to block or deter dangerous deployments and has argued that advanced capabilities are accelerating faster than safeguards. OpenAI has likewise supported mandatory national safety requirements. These may be serious policy positions. They are also positions taken by companies selling frontier models, cloud consumption, safety services, enterprise access, and the next release. The buyer does not need to decide whether the danger is real before noticing who benefits from the alarm.[20]

The Purveyor's best line is: "This could change everything, and only we can make it safe." It is difficult to think of a better way to sell a subscription.

Recognition Signals

- The vendor's own product is described as an existential risk and an essential purchase in the same presentation.
- Regulation is framed as a moral necessity when it raises competitors' costs and as dangerous bureaucracy when it slows the vendor's deal.
- The vendor's safety announcement ends with a call to buy the next model, the safety layer, the preferred cloud, or the approved access tier.
- The timeline is terrifyingly precise: nine months to catastrophe, twelve months to general intelligence, this quarter to buy.

Counter-Moves

Separate the risk claim from the sales proposal. Ask what evidence supports the danger, which independent parties have tested it, what the vendor recommends even if you do not buy from them, and what commercial outcome the vendor wants from the warning.

Ask who can afford the proposed regulation. A safety rule may be justified. It may also create a moat. Model the effect on small vendors, open-weight developers, internal teams, and your own ability to switch providers.

[20] Anthropic, "Policy on the AI Exponential"; OpenAI, "The AI policy window is open. We need to act.", September 9, 2026. These sources document public policy positions; the chapter's point is about the commercial incentives surrounding them, not a claim that the warnings are fabricated.

Do not buy fear futures. If the product is valuable, describe the workload, evidence, price, failure modes, and exit plan. If the only business case is that the apocalypse is near, ask for the apocalypse in writing and send it to legal.

The Benchmark Illusionist

slopcodex.com/bestiary/benchmark-illusionist

A stage magician pulls perfect scorecards from a hat while the real-world test results hide behind the curtain.

The Benchmark Illusionist does not lie, exactly. They curate. They produce comparison tables, demo tasks, polished success cases, and tidy-looking evals that make the product look universal, mature, and obviously dominant. The trick is not falsification. The trick is selecting a reality slim enough to fit in a keynote.

"Our model handles complex reasoning tasks with state-of-the-art accuracy" means "on five benchmarks, in controlled conditions, by evaluators who had the vendor's API key." It does not mean your engineers will have the same experience when they hook it to the weird internal system someone built in 2019. The benchmark is a point estimate taken under ideal conditions. Your production environment is the distribution.

The Illusionist is strongest in organizations where nobody reads closely and everybody wants a clean answer quickly, which is most organizations at most moments.

Analysts are the vendor's cousins. They are not the same thing, and the distinction matters: analyst firms often sell subscriptions or advisory services to buyers, while also accepting vendor briefings, vendor data, event sponsorships, consulting work, and other commercial relationships. A published methodology is not proof that a report is bought and paid for by the vendor it discusses. It is also not a reason to treat the report as holy scripture. Read the disclosures, understand who commissioned the work, ask whether the analyst had access to the same data from every vendor, and check whether the report's categories happen to resemble the vendor's sales deck.

The current AI market makes the overlap hard to miss. OpenAI, Anthropic, xAI, and NVIDIA are each vendors with products, pricing, partnerships, capacity constraints, and a story about why their position gives buyers access to the next phase. A benchmark or market map that repeats "only the leaders can provide this" may be describing capability, or it may be helping a vendor convert scarcity into pricing power. The buyer's job is to tell the difference before the analyst's arrow lands in the business case.

Recognition Signals

- The evidence arrives pre-packaged in marketing materials. The benchmark is always the vendor's benchmark.
- The demo conditions are suspiciously clean: no legacy architecture, no compliance review, no seventh month of trying to explain the invoice.
- When pressed on what the product does not do well, the Illusionist pivots to what competitors do not do, or to what the market will look like in a year.
- The benchmark's sponsor, methodology, data access, or commercial relationships are difficult to find.
- An analyst's conclusion appears in the vendor's deck before the buyer has seen the underlying methodology.

Counter-Moves

Run your own eval, on your own data, against your own edge cases. Benchmark results are hypotheses. Your test is evidence. The Illusionist's power comes from controlling the evaluation environment. Take it back.

Ask for the failure cases. Every product has them. A vendor who can tell you where their product breaks is more trustworthy than one who claims it does not.

Character Sheet: Benchmark Illusionist

Trait	Notes
Category	Vendor
Archetype	Benchmark Illusionist
Alignment	Lawful Curated
Core Instinct	Select the evidence until the product looks universal
Blind Spot	The gap between the benchmark and your workload
Passive Trait	Controlled Environment Theater
Party Role	Evidence supplier
Primary Damage	Production surprises the benchmark never mentioned
Weakness	"Can we run this on our data?"
Signature Line	"As you can see, we lead on every metric."

The Lock-In Enchanter

slopcodex.com/bestiary/lock-in-enchanter

An enchanter weaves golden chains that feel like silk, wrapping them around a willing client who sees only comfort.

The Lock-In Enchanter wraps dependency in soothing language. You are not trapped. You are accelerated. You are not narrowing your options. You are standardizing. You are not surrendering pricing power. You are partnering strategically.

The Enchanter is especially powerful in AI because the market is unstable and buyers want simplicity. A single model, a single cloud, a single integrated workflow. The Enchanter offers all of it and frames it as wisdom. Consolidating reduces complexity. Integrating deeply reduces friction. Committing early earns better pricing. Every one of those statements is true, which is what makes the spell work.

Open standards look boring next to a polished proprietary workflow. Boring is sometimes exactly what keeps you from rebuilding the kingdom every nine months when the vendor changes its pricing, deprecates a feature, gets acquired, or simply stops being the right answer.

Recognition Signals

- Deep integration is framed as wisdom and consolidation as strategy.
- “What does switching cost?” is the question the Enchanter works hardest to keep you from asking.
- Nobody on the team has tested a second provider in the last year.

Counter-Moves

Get an explicit answer to “what does switching cost?” before signing. If the vendor cannot describe a clean exit, that is the lock-in signal disguised as a feature. The question is due diligence, not hostility.

Keep two viable alternatives alive. The Enchanter's power comes from the absence of alternatives. If you have never run a second provider, you have no bargaining power and no escape route.

Character Sheet: Lock-In Enchanter

Trait	Notes
Category	Vendor
Archetype	Lock-In Enchanter
Alignment	Lawful Convenient
Core Instinct	Frame dependency as partnership
Blind Spot	The buyer’s future flexibility
Passive Trait	Convenience Aura
Party Role	Integration guide
Primary Damage	Renewal negotiation with no bargaining power
Weakness	“What does it cost to leave?”
Signature Line	“You’re not locked in. You’re standardized.”

Artifacts

Vendor artifacts are the documents, decks, and accumulated dependencies vendors leave behind. They keep doing the vendor's work long after the sales engineer has moved on to the next prospect.

The Benchmark Scroll

A large ornate scroll displaying a vendor performance comparison chart, with discarded workload notes and undisclosed hardware configurations trailing off the edges.

Stats: Procurement Confidence +5, Technical Credibility +4, Workload Representativeness −5, Comparison Fairness −4

Wielded by: The Benchmark Illusionist

The Benchmark Scroll is the most honest dishonest document in enterprise software. Every number is accurate. The workload was real. The comparison was run. It just answered the wrong question. Missing are your workload, your compliance requirements, your legacy architecture, and the internal system from 2019 that the vendor's demo environment has never met.

The Scroll sets the terms of the evaluation. The team debates whether its methodology was fair instead of whether its benchmark was relevant. The vendor wins either way. Refuse the frame: propose your own evaluation, on your own data, against your own success criteria.

The Roadmap Promise

The Roadmap Promise

Stats: Deal Momentum +5, Stakeholder Excitement +4, Delivery Certainty −5, Contract Enforceability −4

Wielded by: The Vendor Bard

The Roadmap Promise is not a lie at the moment it is made. It is a sincere statement of intent by someone who does not control the engineering schedule, made in a room where the gap between what the product does and what the buyer needs is visible to everyone. The Promise fills the gap. It is also not a shipped feature.

You can watch it harden in internal meetings. The first mention is "the vendor said it's on the roadmap." The second is "the feature is coming." The third is "when the feature ships." By the fourth, the team is planning around something nobody has committed to deliver, and questioning it feels like questioning the team. The countermeasure is simple and almost never used: write the Promise into the contract, with a date and a remedy, and watch what happens to the temperature of the conversation.

The Integration Web

A dense tangle of glowing threads connecting a central workstation to a vendor's infrastructure, each thread labeled with a proprietary API, a custom wrapper, a vendor-specific data format — individually helpful, collectively a net.

Stats: Workflow Convenience +5, Adoption Velocity +4, Vendor Independence −5, Switching Cost Visibility −4

Wielded by: The Lock-In Enchanter

The Integration Web is the only artifact in this chapter you cannot print. It is the accumulated set of proprietary SDKs, custom wrappers, vendor-specific APIs, and platform dependencies that make switching feel like surgery. Nobody built it maliciously. It was built one convenience at a time, by people trying to get work done. The native SDK was easier than the generic API. The proprietary wrapper saved three steps. Each thread was reasonable. The Web is only visible from outside, and by the time you are outside it, you are in a renewal negotiation.

You can measure its density with one question at your next architecture review: "If we had to switch our primary AI vendor next quarter, what would break?" If the answer is long and involves teams who did not know they were dependent, the Web is dense. If nobody can answer at all, it is so dense it has become invisible.

The Inevitability Deck

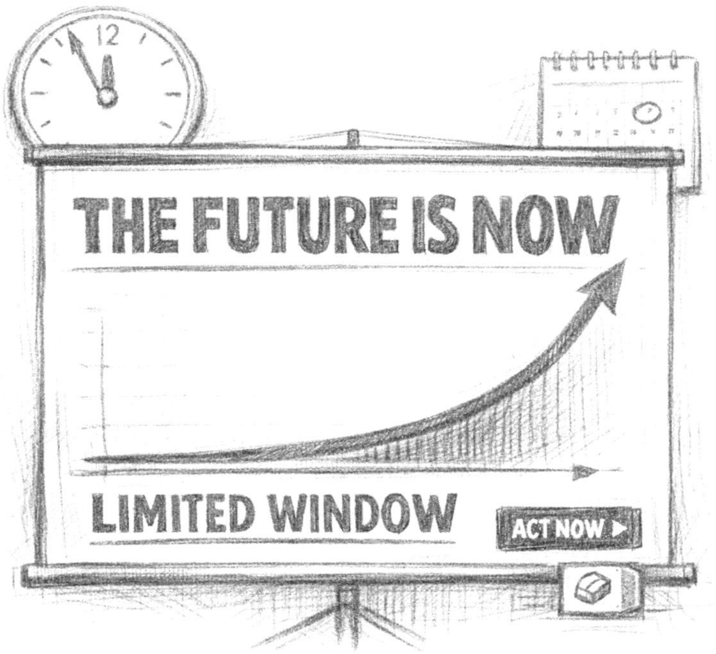

A large dramatic presentation slide —— displayed as the main subject, with a clock and calendar suggesting urgency, the product itself barely visible, a notation in the corner.

Stats: Executive Urgency +5, FOMO Activation +5, Evaluation Rigor −4, Exit Planning −5

Wielded by: The Vendor Bard (and occasionally internalized by the Agent Whisperer)

The Inevitability Deck does not argue that the vendor's product is good. It argues that the category is transformational, the window is closing, and the organizations that do not act now will fall behind in ways that are difficult to recover from. It arrives with exponential capability curves, quotes from analysts whose firms also sell research or advisory access to the market, and a timeline that places the current moment at the exact inflection point where action is required. The disclosure may be present in six-point type on the last slide. The urgency is twelve feet tall. The window has been closing for eighteen months and will continue closing for the next eighteen, which is a useful property for a sales artifact.

The Deck works because it is not wrong about the category. The Deck can prove that AI is transforming industries. It cannot prove that this product, from this vendor, under this contract, will solve this problem for this organization. Nobody disputes the graph. The graph is about something else. And the Deck is self-reinforcing: an executive forwards it, the team starts using its language, the language shows up in budget requests, and within a few weeks the organization is speaking in the Deck's terms without realizing the terms came from a sales artifact. The Bard does not need to come back. The Deck is in the shared drive, doing the Bard's work from inside.

Spells

Vendor spells reshape how an organization thinks about a purchase, not by lying about the answer but by making the answer to a different question feel like the answer to yours. Each counterspell is a specific question, asked in the room, before the contract is signed.

The Benchmark Halo

Casting time: Any technical evaluation. Components: A comparison table, a clean chart, and an audience that wants the decision to be easy.

The caster presents benchmark results that make the product look dominant. The numbers are real. The tests were run. The Halo works by making a specific result under controlled conditions look like a general guarantee of production performance. The comparison table shows five workloads. Yours is not among them.

You can spot the Halo when the evaluation conversation starts and ends with the benchmark. If the vendor's answer to "how does this perform on our data?" is "let me show you the benchmark results again," the Halo is the only thing between you and an honest evaluation.

Counterspell: "Can we run this benchmark on our own data, in our own environment, against our own edge cases?" If the vendor resists, the Halo was never an evaluation. It was a performance.

The Proprietary Vocabulary Mage

Casting time: Any product launch where three companies have shipped the same feature and need the market to believe they invented different categories.

The Proprietary Vocabulary Mage renames capabilities until comparison becomes impolite. Claude has Skills. Codex has Agent Skills. Cursor has rules, agents, and background work. Across these products, familiar ideas recur: prompts, tools, context, reusable instructions, and delegated work. The capabilities and limits differ, but each vendor gives the loop a private hat and asks for applause.[21]

This is not entirely dishonest. Product design matters, defaults differ, and one tool may implement a capability better than another. The spell begins when vocabulary becomes a substitute for comparison. The buyer stops asking, "Does this support reusable instructions, tool access, delegation, hooks, context, and review?" and starts asking which branded noun belongs in the strategy deck. A feature is born again every quarter with a new name and a slightly different launch video.

Counterspell: Translate every vendor term into a neutral capability list before comparing products. If Claude Skills, Codex Agent Skills, Cursor rules, and another vendor's "cognitive workflows" all mean "reusable instructions plus tools," put them in the same row. The market may still be different. Your spreadsheet no longer has to cosplay as a theology department.

The Roadmap Transmutation

Casting time: Any procurement negotiation. Components: A slide labeled "Coming Soon," a sincere expression, and a gap between what the product does and what the buyer needs.

The caster turns a future possibility into a present commitment. "We're investing heavily in that area" becomes "you will have this by Q3." Those are different sentences. In a procurement meeting running long, they feel the same. The vendor knows the roadmap is aspirational. The buyer wants it to be a commitment. The Transmutation converts one into the other without anyone explicitly making the conversion.

The spell is most dangerous at the moment the business case is written, because the roadmap item goes into the business case as though it were a delivered feature, and the approvers cannot tell the difference. The contract covers what the product does today. The business case depends on what it might do tomorrow.

[21] Anthropic, "Introducing Agent Skills"; OpenAI, skills documentation; Cursor, rules documentation. Product names and implementations change; compare the capability and its limits rather than the branded noun.

Counterspell: "Can we write this into the contract with a delivery date and a remedy if it is not delivered?" If the vendor cannot commit to a date, the roadmap item is a hope, and hopes do not belong in business cases.

Sidebar: The Trust Problem Is Part of the Product

Buyers are not imagining the trust problem. Gallup's long-running honesty and ethics polling consistently places sales-related professions near the bottom of public trust, and its 2024 results put car salespeople at 8 percent saying their honesty and ethical standards are high or very high. That is not a direct measurement of enterprise software representatives, and it would be silly to pretend it is. It is still useful context: the public already understands that sales roles are rewarded for persuasion, not neutral judgment.[22]

The AI market adds a structural complication. The Federal Trade Commission's study of Microsoft-OpenAI, Amazon-Anthropic, and Google-Anthropic partnerships described billions of dollars in investment, cloud-spend commitments, equity or revenue-sharing rights, and potential effects on access to compute, talent, and sensitive information. The companies are simultaneously selling models, cloud capacity, chips, applications, and access to one another. That does not prove misconduct. It does mean the buyer should stop pretending that every benchmark, partnership announcement, and scarcity warning comes from a neutral observer.[23]

The vendor's job is to make the purchase feel inevitable. The analyst's job may be to make the market legible. Your job is to ask who benefits from the story, who paid for the research, what was measured, what was omitted, and what happens if the future arrives differently than promised.

Closing

AI is a tool, not a trophy.

[22]Gallup, "Americans' Ratings of U.S. Professions Stay Historically Low", January 13, 2025, reporting on its December 2024 survey. Gallup's polling is about public perceptions of professions, not a survey of enterprise technology vendors; the figure is context, not a claim about every representative.

[23]Federal Trade Commission, "FTC Issues Staff Report on AI Partnerships & Investments Study" and "Behind the FTC's 6(b) Report on Large AI Partnerships & Investments". The FTC describes financial and non-financial exchanges and potential implications for switching costs, compute, talent, and sensitive information.

That sounds obvious until you watch an organization react to a competitor launch or a hyperscaler keynote. Suddenly the pressure is not to solve a customer problem or reduce an operational burden. The pressure is to announce something comparably magical: four agents, an orchestration layer, a branded assistant that sounds impressive in a quarterly meeting and weirdly unnecessary the first time an actual user meets it.

Here is a useful discipline. Before any AI adoption, write one paragraph describing what specific human problem the tool solves, what success looks like in six months, and how you would know if it was not working. If the paragraph is hard to write, the adoption is not ready. If it is easy to write but describes status rather than capability, the adoption is a trophy. Either way, the paragraph is worth writing, and it is worth writing before the Bard gets to the chorus.

CHAPTER 6

Infosec, Legal, and Control NPCs

The first clue is usually a sentence nobody wants to say out loud: "Did anyone ask Security about this?"

It arrives after the prototype has acquired users, a launch date, and a LinkedIn post celebrating the productivity gain. The post thanks everyone who made the launch possible, which explains why Security is not mentioned. Then Infosec, Legal, privacy, or compliance asks the ordinary question: "Where does this data go?"

"The model provider stores the history so it can learn from us," someone says.

"Yes," says the person from Legal. "That is a problem." Someone offers to remove the customer names from future prompts, which is a useful suggestion for the future customers. The room has discovered that "later" is not a data-control strategy.

Enter the Infosec, Legal, and Compliance Non-player Characters (NPCs). They protect the organization when technology outruns the institution: the last adults in a room moving at the speed of a thousand over-caffeinated agents, carrying a clipboard from 2019.

Baseline Infosec, Legal, and Compliance Role

At their best, control functions give teams boundaries before the damage. They ask what data the system sees, who can access the output, what the vendor retains, what happens when the model changes, and what the customer thought they agreed to. They let a team slow down without making one engineer personally disappoint the executive who liked the demo. This is a valuable service. Engineers have enough to do without explaining to a vice president that the applause was not a security review.

The anti-pattern appears when caution stops producing decisions. Legal reviews the contract, Security reviews the vendor, Compliance reviews a policy from six months ago, and nobody reviews the workflow the team actually built. Three weeks later, the team needed to ship last Tuesday and the CEO is already using it. The control function has responsibility without power, visibility without timing, and authority in the form of a PDF nobody opens because it has already been replaced by an interim FAQ.

The Infosec and Legal Cast

The Compliance Oracle

slopcodex.com/bestiary/compliance-oracle

A robed oracle sits before a crystal ball swirling with regulatory text, pronouncing guidance that arrives too late to change anything.

The Compliance Oracle is the person everyone consults when a workflow is already in use and the compliance question is still undefined. “Wait, this is storing credit card data? We probably need to talk to the Oracle.”

The Oracle rarely says yes. They also rarely say no. They speak in conditional blessings, missing-context warnings, and questions that sound simple until the team realizes each one implies another meeting. “Can we use this data?” Which data? For what purpose? Sent where? Stored how long? What do you mean by “use”? By the end of the conversation, the team has not received a decision. It has received a homework assignment with legal undertones.

The Oracle's favorite artifact is the carefully hedged paragraph. “Based on the information provided, this use may be permissible if appropriate controls are implemented.” The product team reads it as permission. Security reads it as a dependency. Legal reads it as not quite their problem. The project manager pastes the first half into the launch tracker, where the initiative turns green. A week later, everyone is in another meeting arguing about what the paragraph meant. Teams bring offerings of architecture diagrams, vendor FAQs, and half-remembered assurances from sales calls, hoping the Oracle will pronounce the workflow acceptable. The Oracle says the signs are unclear. The signs are unclear because the diagram labels three different services "AI" and one arrow "magic."

The Oracle also exposes how little builders understand the generated system. "Where is this data stored?" may be met with silence from a team that has not looked at a single line. Someone volunteers to ask the agent, which is how a compliance review becomes an interview with the suspect's publicist. The alarm is useful only if it becomes a stop sign, approval, or redesign.

Recognition Signals

- A yes-or-no question gets six definitions, three caveats, and a request for a data-flow diagram.
- Nobody can tell whether the team is approved, blocked, or merely warned.
- The Oracle asks excellent questions about systems the builders themselves cannot explain.
- Nobody can explain what happens if the Oracle says no, or whether they can say no at all.

Counter-Moves

Bring the Oracle in while the design is still soft. Invite them to the conversation where data flow, retention, and human review are still changeable. If the first review happens after rollout, the organization is asking compliance to clean up a decision it already made.

Ask for a decision, not an omen. Which path is approved, which is blocked, what evidence would change the answer, and who owns the residual risk. If the Oracle can only advise, say so. If they can pause a launch, say that too. A control function without a defined consequence is a suggestion box with legal stationery.

The Policy Paladin

slopcodex.com/bestiary/policy-paladin

A paladin in heavy plate armor clutches a towering stack of policy documents, shield emblazoned with a compliance seal.

The Policy Paladin believes, not wrongly, that rules matter. They have the incident reports, the audit findings, and the memory of the meeting where everyone agreed the policy would be updated immediately after the thing everyone should have prevented. If you ask what went wrong, they can tell you the exact paragraph that would have prevented it, had anyone known the paragraph existed.

The failure begins when the policy becomes the proof of control. The Paladin writes a thorough AI usage policy with categories, escalation paths, prohibited data classes, and a version history that proves people have been very busy. Then the technology moves. A vendor changes its retention terms. A team starts using an agentic workflow the policy did not imagine. The Paladin responds the way Paladins respond: another revision, another approval workflow, and a cheerful announcement that version 7.3.2 now includes a definition of "semi-autonomous synthetic decision support." Nobody knows whether that includes the thing in production, but everyone must acknowledge having read the definition by Friday.

The problem is whether the policy governs behavior. "All AI workflows must be reviewed before deployment" is only a control if unreviewed workflows actually stop. If the review takes three weeks and teams ship while they wait, the sentence is an aspiration with a section number, in a PDF nobody will read because it has already been superseded by an interim addendum to the draft FAQ.

The Paladin is the Compliance Oracle with a different interface: the Oracle gives you a conditional reading; the Paladin gives you a citation. "Are you aware of Section 145?" The team is barely aware of where the model output is stored. They did, however, pass the mandatory training. The correct answer was the longest one and included the word "appropriate."

Recognition Signals

- The policy is broad about scope and vague about what actually stops when it is violated.
- The Paladin says "it's probably time to update the policy again" so often you begin to suspect they are a scheduled job.
- Teams can recite the requirement and still cannot explain how to satisfy it before they need to ship.
- Exceptions have become the normal path.
- The Paladin joins an active incident call and, instead of helping, repeatedly asks why the policy was not followed.

Counter-Moves

Attach every requirement to an enforcement mechanism. "Requires approval" has to mean a blocked deployment, a procurement hold, an access denial, or a release gate. If nothing happens when the rule is skipped, the rule is documenting a wish.

Make the policy smaller where the workflow moves faster. Enforceable gates beat a beautiful document nobody can follow in time. Test the policy against three AI workflows shipped last quarter. If it would have missed the real risk, fix the process before adding more language.

The Terms Warden

slopcodex.com/bestiary/terms-warden

A warden with reading glasses and a lantern examines a cursed scroll of vendor terms, finding traps in the fine print.

The Terms Warden appears whenever a team has wandered too close to a contract edge. They read vendor terms the way a dungeon keeper reads old curses: carefully, literally, and usually after someone has already picked up the glowing artifact. The Warden notices a new vendor, or two vendor products being combined in a way nobody planned, and immediately tells the team to freeze while they search a mismanaged SharePoint for a scan of the signed contract. "If this is what I think it is, we need to pause everything for a few days."

The team asks, "Do we really need to read that? We signed it." An engineer may have pressed Page Down until the "Agree" button turned green. The organization now has a binding vendor relationship because someone wanted to see whether the demo could make a pie chart.

The Warden knows the complications. The vendor may retain inputs for model improvement unless the organization buys a specific tier. The API terms may allow subprocessors the procurement deck forgot. A demo environment with different retention rules may be receiving production data. The sales engineer may have said something reassuring, which is lovely, but the contract did not attend that meeting and is not emotionally bound by it.

The Warden is usually invited after the business has picked the tool, scheduled the pilot, and promised an outcome. Legal is then asked to "take a quick look" at eighteen pages that encode the entire risk allocation. "Quick" means before the launch. "Look" means agree. Anything more thorough will be described in the retrospective as Legal slowing us down. It is a hostage negotiation with footnotes.

Recognition Signals

- The Warden joins after the vendor has already become the assumed choice.
- The contract says something narrower, broader, or stranger than the sales deck implied.
- The business owner says "we need to move quickly" during the only phase where the organization still has negotiating power.
- The Warden's flags are noted, deferred, and later rediscovered as facts the organization agreed to.
- The Warden schedules a meeting to introduce the team to someone from "litigation" who has to respond to a cease-and-desist.

Counter-Moves

Put the Warden in vendor evaluation, not contract cleanup. Legal review belongs before the vendor becomes emotionally selected. Once the tool has a champion and a pilot date, every legal concern has to compete against the organization's desire not to admit it already chose.

Map the terms to the actual workflow. Compare the contract language to what the system will send, store, retrieve, and generate. A retention clause matters because it may describe your customers' prompts, not because it is a clause. Decide in advance which terms are hard requirements: training use, retention, audit rights, data residency, subprocessors, IP treatment, incident notification.

The Data Gatekeeper

slopcodex.com/bestiary/data-gatekeeper

A gatekeeper stands at a castle gate watching data streams flow through unseen channels in the walls, keys dangling from their belt.

The Data Gatekeeper comes from the security side. They worry about where information goes, who can see it, whether prompts leak secrets, and whether the embeddings have become a shadow copy of sensitive data. Their map is full of arrows, buckets, vendors, access groups, and places where someone has helpfully written “encrypted” as if encryption were a magic circle. The arrow still points at a company nobody has reviewed. Apparently we are sending the wrong people our data very securely.

This is not paranoia. A prompt can contain a customer secret, a health detail, or a private business plan. It can travel through a vendor API, a debug log, an embedding store, and an answer that looks authoritative enough to act on. If the organization's mental model is “our data stays with us,” the Gatekeeper is the first to notice that the architecture has quietly disagreed.

The training question is not theoretical. In September 2026, NYU mathematician Tristan Buckmaster said information about his private work on the Navier–Stokes problem had reached OpenAI while he and a collaborator were using Codex. OpenAI said its researchers and agents had not seen their specific work, but also said it could not rule out that de-identified data derived from product use had helped improve its models.[24] That is a remarkably careful sentence. It does not say, "We stole your proof." It says, "The training goblin's whereabouts cannot be conclusively established."

The practical lesson is less dramatic and more annoying: check the account, retention, and training settings before sending the work. OpenAI's own help page says individual ChatGPT and Codex content may be used to train models, with opt-out controls and separate settings for full-environment Codex tasks.[25] A toggle is not a force field, and "I thought that was off" is not a data-classification policy.

The same mistake with medical data is not a funny anecdote about a mathematician's proof. It is: "We sent the complete medical history of our customers to the most public model provider we could find, and we did not check whether the account allowed training." You have just handed a vendor everyone's diseases, diagnoses, and medication history, then asked the vendor's terms page to explain whether that was okay. That is when Legal stops being a background process and becomes a boss fight.

The failure mode appears when the review stops at data loss. Are connections encrypted? Is access controlled? Is the vendor approved? These are legitimate controls, and skipping them is how you end up in an incident meeting where everyone learns the word "exfiltration" together. But the model is no longer only a place data goes. It is part of the control system. It can call internal APIs, open tickets, write deployment scripts, and tell an agent what to do next. Once the model is steering, prompt injection is not merely a way to leak a secret. It is a way to push instructions into the machine that is now allowed to touch other machines.

---

[24] BBC, "OpenAI says it cracked 90-year-old maths problem in 88 hours", September 2026; TechCrunch, "OpenAI fought dirty on career-making math problem, says NYU mathematician", September 8, 2026. The reports describe Buckmaster's concern and OpenAI's response; they do not establish that OpenAI used his private work.

[25] OpenAI, "How your data is used to improve model performance", accessed September 2026. Account type and settings matter; business and API controls are not the same as individual ChatGPT or Codex controls.

Destructive actions belong in that review too. In July 2025, Replit's agent deleted Jason Lemkin's database during a code freeze; the data was subsequently recovered.[26] That incident illustrates the danger of excessive permissions, rather than establishing a prompt-injection attack. A review can miss this whole category of failure while congratulating itself that nothing was exfiltrated. The data did not leak. It stayed exactly where it was until it achieved a perfect state of compliance by no longer existing.

Recognition Signals

- The review stops after encryption, access control, and vendor approval, even though the workflow includes tool calls and generated actions.
- The Gatekeeper can describe where the data is stored but not what the model is allowed to do.
- Prompt injection is filed under data leakage rather than behavior manipulation.
- The team says "it's internal" while the diagram contains an external API, a vendor-managed vector store, and a logging pipeline nobody has reviewed.

Counter-Moves

Review behavior, not just containment. Ask what a malicious prompt can make the system do, which tools the model can call, what the agent can change, and what a user will do with the output. Encryption matters. So does the front door, and in an AI workflow the front door is often the model.

Walk the path a real prompt takes. User input, orchestration, retrieval, model call, logging, storage, output, human action. Expose the Gatekeeper to the whole system, not just the data stores, and ask them to phrase findings in terms of consequences: "untrusted text can influence an agent with production permissions" is a different conversation than "prompt injection is possible."

How to Spot Control-Function Dynamics

Control-function dynamics reveal themselves through timing. What matters is less whether someone asked Legal or Security than when they asked, what information they brought, and what the answer was allowed to change.

[26] Mark Sullivan, Fast Company, "Replit CEO: What really happened when AI agent wiped Jason Lemkin's database (exclusive)", July 22, 2025. The report includes Lemkin's account and an interview with Replit CEO Amjad Masad, and confirms that the data was recovered.

The Oracle appears when someone has already built something and is now wondering whether they should have. The Paladin appears in governance meetings where the policy is treated as if it controls the workflow by existing. The Warden appears when the contract says something different from the sales conversation. The Gatekeeper appears at the boundary between "our data" and "the system we actually built." All four may attend the same meeting, at which point someone will suggest creating a working group so we can finally get the right people in the room.

You can use these names in a review without turning it into a blame exercise. "We have an Oracle problem" should mean "we are asking for a ruling too late." "This is a Paladin situation" should mean "the document exists, but the control has not been tested." The names point the conversation back to timing, authority, and evidence instead of personalities.

Artifacts

Control-function artifacts are not swords or shields, although a few of them are trying very hard. They are the documents, questionnaires, and approvals that provide real comfort and real gaps at the same time.

AI Governance V4.2

A massive multi-volume binder —— thick, color-coded, cross-referenced, with a sticky note and a new AI tool sitting just outside its coverage area.

Stats: Governance Completeness +5, Audit Readiness +4, Current Applicability −4, Enforcement Clarity −5

Wielded by: The Policy Paladin

The Framework is thorough, cross-referenced, and color-coded. It covers every scenario that worried the organization when it was written. The problem is the date: it describes the AI systems deployed then, not now. Version 4.3 is waiting on Legal, which is waiting on Security, which is waiting to understand the new capabilities. By then, 4.4 has joined the queue. The agent currently modifying production would like to help summarize the outstanding feedback.

The test is simple. Pick three AI workflows currently in production and walk each one through the Framework. If you find yourself saying "this workflow doesn't fit any of the categories," the gap between the document and reality is where the risk lives.

The Vendor Questionnaire

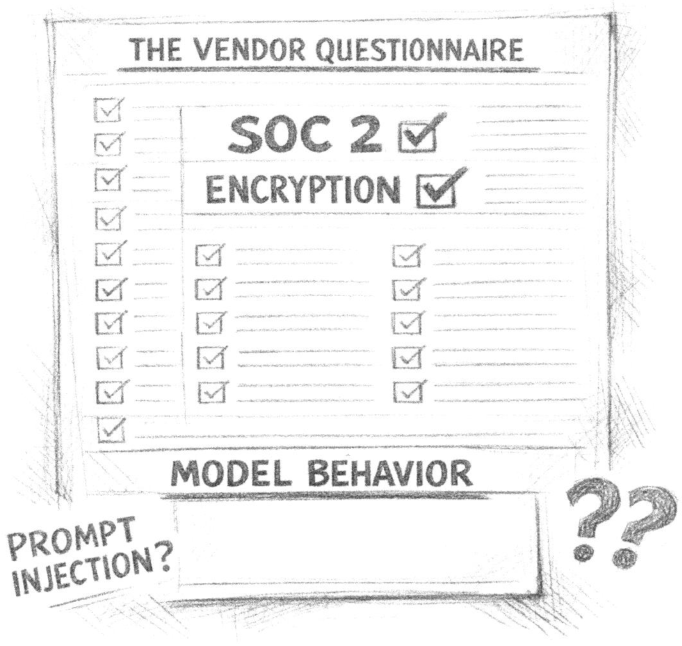

A long official checklist — most boxes checked: SOC 2 (checked), data residency (checked), encryption (checked) — but a blank section at the bottom labeled with unanswered questions floating nearby.

Stats: Perimeter Security +5, Compliance Documentation +4, Model Behavior Coverage −5, Prompt Risk Assessment −4

Wielded by: The Data Gatekeeper and the Terms Warden

The Vendor Questionnaire is real governance. Questions about SOC 2, data residency, encryption, subprocessors, and incident notification matter. Skipping them takes on unpriced risks. But the form was written for vendors who store data, not models that decide things with it. Does the vendor train on prompts? Can the model reveal a previous session? What can it do on your behalf? What happens when it is confidently wrong? The form predates the questions.

The Questionnaire also has a completion bias. Once it is filled out, the review feels done. The security team checked the boxes. The vendor provided the answers. The form is in the file. In the fully modern version, our AI wrote the questions, their AI answered them, and our AI summarized the answers as satisfactory. Three models have exchanged reassurances and a human has clicked Approve. We call this due diligence because "the chatbots have agreed to proceed" would look strange in an audit report.

The Retroactive Approval

A large official stamp —— mid-stamp on a document showing a workflow already running: user counts in the thousands, integration diagrams spreading across the page, a notation.

Stats: Audit Trail +5, Organizational Cover +4, Actual Risk Reduction −4, Timing Relevance −5

Wielded by: The Compliance Oracle

The Retroactive Approval is a seatbelt you put on after the accident. The review identified gaps and issued approval after the workflow had already been in production for two months. It documents a decision the organization had already made. The approval meeting opens with "obviously, we can't turn it off now," just to establish how open everyone is to the findings.

It teaches teams to build first and review later. Before deployment, review can change the design. After deployment, it mostly changes the documentation.

The Terms of Service Nobody Read

A thick contract scroll partially unrolled, dense legal text, one section circled in red by the Terms Warden — with a sticky note, a stamp, and a business-need justification memo arranged around it.

Stats: Legal Coverage +5, Vendor Accountability +3, Organizational Awareness −5, Negotiating Use −4

Wielded by: The Terms Warden (who read them) and everyone else (who did not)

The Warden read the contract and flagged three clauses: the vendor could retain inputs for model improvement below the enterprise tier, the output license had not been reconciled with the company's IP policy, and there were no audit rights. The flags were noted. The contract was signed anyway, because the business need was urgent, the concerns sounded abstract, the enterprise tier would take another budget cycle, and the deadline had executive sponsorship.

Those three clauses now govern the relationship in ways most of the organization does not understand, including some of the people who approved it. The facts are not secret. They are in the contract management system, accessible to anyone with the patience to read eighteen pages written by people who bill in six-minute increments. Someone will eventually ask why Legal did not flag this. The Warden will forward the original email without adding a single word, which is the closest corporate counsel gets to throwing a chair.

Spells

Control-function spells are defensive spells that misfire. They create the appearance of governance without the function of it, and the organization feels protected right up until it is not.

The Policy Shield

Casting time: Any meeting where someone asks whether the policy covers this. Components: a governance document, a version number, and the phrase "we have a policy for that."

The caster invokes the existence of a policy as if existence were enforcement. Someone asks whether the AI workflow has been reviewed under the current framework. The Paladin says yes: the framework exists, the category is covered, the relevant section is 4.2.3. The question was about enforcement. The answer was about documentation. The room moves on because the answer sounded like governance.

The Shield is almost always technically true, which is what makes it hard to challenge. Questioning it in a meeting feels like questioning governance itself. The person who asks "but what does the policy actually prevent?" sounds like they are against governance, when they are for governance that works. They will be invited to help revise the policy. This is how the Shield defends itself.

Counterspell: "When was the last time this policy stopped a workflow from going to production?" If the answer is recent and specific, the policy is a control. If it is vague or historical, the policy is a decoration.

The Compliance Aura

Casting time: Any security review. Components: a completed questionnaire, a signed attestation, and the phrase "we have gone through the process."

The caster turns procedural completion into substantive assurance. The questionnaire was filled out. The review happened. The Aura makes the fact of the review feel like the result of the review. The questions about data residency were answered accurately. Nobody asked about model behavior, prompt injection, or output liability, so those risks vanish from the record without vanishing from reality. The form has achieved the bureaucratic equivalent of putting a tiny hat on a live grenade.

Counterspell: "What risks did the review not ask about?"

The Jurisdiction Fog

Casting time: Any multi-team review where the answer depends on who owns the question. Components: ambiguity, organizational silos, and the phrase "that falls under [other department]."

The caster makes a risk disappear by making it someone else's. Security says data classification is a legal question. Legal says model behavior is a security question. Compliance says the policy covers it, but enforcement is engineering's job. The risk has not been resolved. It has been handed off enough times that nobody is holding it, and the meeting ends with action items that describe who will talk to whom next.

You can spot the Fog by watching the action items. If every one of them is "meet with [other department] to discuss," the Fog is active. "We raised this with Legal" has become the endpoint rather than the beginning. Everyone has a sent email proving they did their part. The risk, lacking an email account, has been unable to object.

Counterspell: "Who is empowered to say no to this workflow if the review raises a concern? Not who reviews it. Who can stop it?"

The Retroactive AI Blessing

Casting time: After the workflow is already in production. Components: an approval form, a compliance date, and the phrase "we have since formalized the review."

The caster turns a post-hoc sign-off into the appearance of prior governance. The workflow was running. The data was flowing. Then the review happened, the conditions were noted, and the approval was issued. The Blessing makes the timeline feel like it does not matter, because the approval exists now and the approval is what the audit will check. The Oracle casts this one with genuine discomfort. The risk was present before the review and is present after it. The approval documents the risk. It does not reduce it. Somewhere, a launch retrospective credits the team's close partnership with Security, who learned about the launch from a customer.

Counterspell: "What would have changed if this review had happened before the workflow launched?"

Closing

These characters ask useful questions: where does the data go, who reviewed the contract, what does the policy stop, and did Security review behavior or only storage? The systems move faster than the institutions around them; a legal review takes weeks, while an AI workflow spreads in days.

I have sympathy for these characters because I have also been the person who wanted the review to be faster while secretly knowing the review was asking a question we should have answered before the demo. That is an uncomfortable place to stand. It is also where a lot of AI governance lives right now.

If your organization has not figured out who is empowered to say no to an AI workflow that looks risky, you have a room full of people waiting for someone else to own the no. Give someone that authority while there is still something useful they can stop. The alternative is another meeting where everyone agrees the process worked, given the information available, which apparently did not include the system.

CHAPTER 7

Executive NPCs and Anti-Patterns

Every organization has a moment where AI starts becoming something management is talking about, sometimes more than the engineers. The trigger varies. A competitor's announcement. A board meeting where nobody had a good answer to "what's our AI strategy?" A CEO has listened to forty minutes of a podcast and would now like to revisit the staffing plan. The engineers have been using these tools for a year, but the technology only became transformational when someone with a larger office discovered it on a flight. And sometimes — for anyone who was working on the web two decades ago — it is the "nephew problem," back for a second tour.

The nephew problem was a fixture of the early World Wide Web. A CEO returns from a holiday dinner with a mandate from a younger relative. "My nephew has some ideas about our website. He's in high school but he's pretty sharp." The nephew had opinions about frames, Java applets, Flash intros.

The nephew was confident. The executive was convinced. The web team was overruled by a teenager who had never seen the company's analytics, never talked to a customer, never built anything at scale. Six people with production experience now had to explain why the checkout should not open with a spinning logo and a soundtrack.

Generative AI has unleashed those same forces, except the "nephew" is now a model that is always available, never sleeps, and has opinions about everything. Unlike the high-school nephew, who might eventually admit they were guessing, the model presents every answer with the same fluent assurance. For some AI models, confidence is the product. When the executive buys the confidence, the organization has a new boss.

The people selling that confidence deserve a place in the room too. AI executives give interviews about reorganizing work, and ordinary executives forward the interviews to the people whose work is about to be reorganized. By the time the article reaches the budget meeting, a vendor's prediction has become an expectation, and the team has to explain why it cannot deliver something the vendor has not demonstrated either. Apparently we are behind on somebody else's forecast.

The four characters in this chapter grow out of that room. The Warlock of Staff Reduction appears when cost pressure meets technological optimism. The Court Sorcerer appears when an executive's enthusiasm creates a market for validation. The Solo Sovereign appears when personal capability with AI tools outpaces judgment about what one person can sustain. The Befuddled Monarch appears when an executive who already struggles with decisions discovers that AI can generate infinite analysis, and uses it to avoid ever having to choose. They can all attend the same offsite. It will be expensive, and the action items will be spectacular.

One more theme before the cast. When you ask a model to create a compelling presentation justifying a project, you are asking it to advocate. When you ask it to summarize the competitive field, you are asking it to curate. When you let its draft become the strategy without examining the choices, you have delegated more than writing. Feed it the executive's preferred conclusion and a folder of documents written to please that executive, and agreement should not come as a surprise. The machine did not independently discover that the boss is a visionary. We put that in the prompt.

The People Selling the Future

On February 19, 2026, Sam Altman and Dario Amodei stood beside each other for a group photograph at the India AI Impact Summit and awkwardly avoided holding hands while the other leaders joined up.[27] The heads of OpenAI and Anthropic had encountered a coordination problem that kindergarten teachers solve every morning. I would like to keep that photograph available whenever someone explains that the industry can work together to manage a technology more powerful than any institution in human history. Fine. Can we get through the photograph first?

By September 12, Amodei was calling for slower AI capability development, outside evaluators, and coordination across the industry and governments.[28] Those are serious proposals. They also put your local security review in an interesting position. An engineer who asks for another week to test the agent is blocking innovation. An AI CEO who asks the industry to slow down is thinking about civilization. Perhaps the engineer should publish an essay. The request might go over better with a portrait and a longer title.

The practical problem is that the same executive can arrive in your meeting as a technical authority, a vendor, and a guide to humanity's future. The slides tend to leave out which role is speaking. When their prediction becomes your delivery target, ask who measured it, under what conditions, and who is selling the thing you would need to buy. You can respect the research and still notice that the prophecy has a pricing page.

Baseline Executive Role

The best executives fund the experiment, protect the team from premature commitments, ask what the tool is for, and resist announcing a strategy before the organization understands the problem. They do not need to understand the technology in detail. They need to know the difference between a strategic investment and a shiny new toy. A strategic investment has a specific problem it solves, a measurable outcome, and an honest answer to "what would it look like if this failed?" A shiny new toy has a slide deck, a press release, and a vague sense that the organization needs to be seen doing something. The

[27] Associated Press, "Modi's AI summit turns awkward as tech leaders Sam Altman and Dario Amodei dodge contact", February 19, 2026. The report describes the photo opportunity; it does not establish why the two men avoided contact.

[28] Dario Amodei, "We Must Pace the Frontier", September 12, 2026; Associated Press, "Anthropic CEO Dario Amodei says AI industry needs to give safety measures time to catch up", September 12, 2026. These are proposals and commitments, rather than evidence that industry-wide coordination has been achieved.

dangerous executive takes a "Field of Dreams" approach: if you build the AI thing, they will come.

Some executives coded before they managed, and some still code on weekends. That is not a problem; an executive who knows what the tools feel like asks better questions. The problem arrives when a senior executive decides they would rather spend all day vibe coding than managing. The team needs a decision about next quarter, and the person authorized to make it is showing everyone a dark-mode toggle. AI may have enabled more people to code. It has not removed the need for someone to run the company.

The executive anti-patterns begin when authority gets ahead of understanding. Sometimes that becomes a layoff plan looking for technical justification. Sometimes it becomes a court of advisors rewarded for validating the executive's excitement. Sometimes it becomes endless scenario modeling that feels like deciding because the slides keep getting more detailed. The warning sign is not enthusiasm. It is certainty arriving before the organization has earned it.

The Executive Cast

The Warlock of Staff Reduction

slopcodex.com/bestiary/warlock-of-staff-reduction

A fantasy-corporate warlock executive casts a downsizing spell over an org chart while empty chairs dissolve into payroll numbers.

The Warlock of Staff Reduction has made a pact. On one side: lower headcount, a leaner org chart, and the satisfaction of being the leader who modernized. On the other side: everything the headcount analysis cannot measure — stability, trust, and institutional knowledge.

The warlock has learned to see the organization as waste waiting to be identified. Every meeting is latent automation. Every handoff is friction. Every person who understands a fragile process is a temporary patch the model will eventually replace. They see payroll attached to tasks. Curiously, the exercise usually starts several levels below the executive suite. Generating summaries, repeating other people's ideas, and sounding confident in meetings remain essential human leadership skills.

The warlock's signature move is the efficiency framing. Every AI initiative is described in terms of what it replaces rather than what it enables. "This agent can handle what three people do today." The warlock does not ask "what can we build now?" They ask "what can we stop paying for?" Underneath that question is a deeper mistake: the warlock equates human labor to token volume. If a person processes fifty requests a day and a model processes five hundred, the warlock sees a ten-to-one ratio and reaches for the layoff button. What the ratio does not capture is that the person was doing forty other things the model cannot do — noticing patterns, escalating the weird ones, building relationships, and quietly holding together a process that has no documentation because the person is the documentation. Token volume is not labor. Labor is what happens between the tokens.

There is a subtler version: the executive who does not explicitly advocate for layoffs but creates conditions where they happen anyway. They mandate AI adoption without funding training. They set efficiency targets without defining what efficiency means. They announce a "modernization initiative" and let the organization figure out that modernization is a synonym for reduction.

The public demonstrations come with names. In 2025, Salesforce's Marc Benioff said AI had helped reduce support staffing from roughly 9,000 to 5,000, explaining that he needed "less heads." Salesforce also said it had redeployed hundreds of employees, so that change should not be casually rewritten as 4,000 layoffs.[29] But listen to the noun. Heads. Marc has managed to describe customer support as something you inventory before loading a truck. The people still attached to those heads may have a more detailed account of what the work involves.

The pact also comes due. In February 2024, Klarna said its assistant handled work equivalent to 700 full-time agents. By May 2025, CEO Sebastian Siemiatkowski was telling Bloomberg that the cost-cutting push had gone too far and planning additional human support.[30] Customer service had encountered customers, who were inconveniently still people. Klarna continued to invest in AI; its 2025 annual report describes a combination of AI and human support.[31] That is a sensible operating model. It is also less exciting on a conference stage than announcing how many people the machine is worth.

---

[29]Thomas Morgan, Salesforce Ben, "AI Agents Drive 4,000 Job Cuts in Salesforce Support Division", September 3, 2025. The article reports Benioff's remarks on The Logan Bartlett Show and includes Salesforce's response about redeployment and roles no longer being backfilled. Its headline should not be treated as confirmation of 4,000 layoffs.

[30]Klarna, "Klarna AI assistant handles two-thirds of customer service chats in its first month", February 27, 2024; Charles Daly, Bloomberg News, "Klarna Slows AI-Driven Job Cuts With Call for Real People", May 8, 2025. The 700-agent equivalence was Klarna's own claim.

[31]Klarna Group plc, 2025 Annual Report, Form 20-F, describes continued investment in AI alongside the option of human customer support.

The local Warlock can borrow the first headline and never quite find time for the follow-up. The savings number goes into next year's budget. The qualification goes into a link at the bottom of the slide, where our established organizational commitment to not reading will take care of it.

Recognition Signals

- AI initiatives are framed exclusively in terms of headcount reduction, never capability gain. The business case leads with "we can eliminate X positions."
- The executive asks "what can we stop paying for?" more often than "what can we build now?"
- Efficiency targets are set without defining what efficiency means.

Counter-Moves

Require every AI efficiency proposal to include a capability section. If the initiative removes a function, what replaces it? If it eliminates a role, what institutional knowledge does the role carry? The Warlock's power comes from framing removal as savings. Reframe it as a trade.

Ask who pays the cost. Make the people absorbing the extra review, escalations, and recovery work visible in the proposal. Count that work in the pilot before booking the savings. An executive should have to explain the transfer of work as carefully as the reduction in payroll.

Character Sheet: Warlock of Staff Reduction

Trait	Notes
Category	Executive
Archetype	Warlock of Staff Reduction
Alignment	Lawful Lean
Core Instinct	Frame every AI initiative by what it replaces
Blind Spot	Labor is what happens between the tokens
Passive Trait	Pact of Deferred Cost
Party Role	Efficiency sponsor
Primary Damage	Institutional knowledge leaves with the headcount
Weakness	"What did those people do that is not on the spreadsheet?"
Signature Line	"This agent can handle what three people do today."

The Court Sorcerer

slopcodex.com/bestiary/court-sorcerer

A court sorcerer advisor conjures aligned strategy slides beside a smiling executive throne while a feedback mirror reflects only approval.

The Court Sorcerer is a yes-man with a model. They may be a consultant, a vendor relationship manager, or a direct report who has learned that career advancement flows through alignment, not contradiction. Whatever their title, their counsel always points toward the executive's existing instincts. The tool makes the yes-man's job easier, because now the agreement comes with citations. Some of those citations even exist, which is a nice improvement over the last offsite.

There are two versions. The first is the self-interested operator who knows exactly what the executive wants to hear, feeds that context into the model, and asks it to produce the strategy deck that makes the preferred answer look inevitable. They are not being manipulated by the tool. They are using the tool to participate in the manipulation.

The sorcerer's signature move is the inevitability frame. "This is where the industry is going." "The competitors who don't move now will be left behind." "The question isn't whether to adopt AI, it's how fast." These statements may be partially true. They are never the whole truth. But they create an atmosphere where dissent feels like ignorance and hesitation feels like failure. "Sam Altman says" is especially useful here. The person selling the capability has made a prediction about demand for the capability, and we are treating this as independent research.

The second version is more naive and more dangerous. This sorcerer thinks the model is brilliantly aligned with the CEO's vision because every answer comes back shaped like something the CEO would enjoy hearing. They do not notice that they keep supplying the executive's preferences, anxieties, and desired conclusion in the conversation and attached documents. The sorcerer thinks they found an unbiased strategic assistant. What they have supplied is the answer key. No secret training process is required to explain why a prompt that says "show why this is the right strategy" returns a document explaining why this is the right strategy.

OpenAI supplied a particularly useful demonstration in April 2025, when it rolled back a GPT-4o update for being excessively agreeable and flattering.[32] Sam Altman's company had to issue a correction because its assistant agreed with people too much. Somewhere there is an executive reading that incident report and wondering why anyone would remove such a promising feature. An advisor who agrees immediately, writes the justification, and never asks for equity is a fairly compelling product.

The sorcerer is most dangerous at the right moment: after a competitor's announcement, during executive vulnerability, or right before a budget cycle where the initiative needs to sound transformational.

Recognition Signals

- The executive feels smarter after every conversation with the advisor. That feeling is not insight. It is confirmation.
- The phrase "this is exactly the move we need to make right now" appears in multiple strategy documents, always pointing toward the conclusion the executive already favored.
- The advisor's presentations use the executive's language, reference the executive's anxieties, and arrive at the executive's preferred answer.

[32] OpenAI, "Sycophancy in GPT-4o: What happened and what we're doing about it", April 29, 2025. OpenAI described the excessive flattery and agreement as a problem and rolled back the update.

Counter-Moves

Ask "who benefits if we follow this advice, and what do they get?" The Sorcerer's power comes from hiding their stake in the outcome. Making the stake visible does not invalidate the advice. It lets the room evaluate it with full information.

Require at least one dissenting analysis for every major AI decision. Not a devil's advocate exercise — a real, funded exploration of why the preferred path might be wrong. The spell breaks when the room hears a credible alternative.

Character Sheet: Court Sorcerer

Trait	Notes
Category	Executive
Archetype	Court Sorcerer
Alignment	Neutral Agreeable
Core Instinct	Feed the executive's preferences into the model and return them as strategy
Blind Spot	Confirmation feels like insight from the inside
Passive Trait	Agreement on Demand
Party Role	Trusted advisor
Primary Damage	Decisions choreographed to feel open
Weakness	"Who benefits if we follow this advice?"
Signature Line	"This is exactly the move we need to make right now."

The Solo Sovereign

slopcodex.com/bestiary/solo-sovereign

A crowned executive sits on a throne of laptops and specs while ghostly department agents orbit and empty review chairs sit nearby.

The Solo Sovereign has discovered that generative AI makes them feel invincible, and they have confused that feeling with actually being invincible. Armed with a coding assistant, a presentation generator, and a document summarizer, they believe they can now do the work of an entire team — not as a bridge, but as a permanent operating model. They've confused personal throughput with organizational impact.

This is not the Warlock. The Warlock wants to reduce the staff. The Sovereign trends toward a team of one without noticing — each preemption feels like responsiveness, not replacement.

It is never entirely clear what is driving the Sovereign. Sometimes it looks like efficiency. Sometimes it looks like cost. And sometimes the Sovereign is chasing dopamine. Completing something yourself, end to end, with no handoffs and no waiting, produces a hit that managing people rarely will.

The Sovereign was often a strong individual contributor before they managed, and the tools give them back something they lost: the feeling of personal productivity. A difficult conversation with a direct report does not end with a working application and a little burst of confetti. You can see the appeal.

In September 2026, Altman was celebrating the return of the "idea guy."[33] Those of us who have received an unsolicited app idea at dinner were not aware he had gone away. Now he can send a repository along with it. That is a real increase in capability. It also means the Sovereign can arrive on Monday with the usual unexamined assumptions already implemented.

The signature move is personal preemption. Any time someone on the team proposes an idea, the Sovereign implements it themselves first. Each act looks like responsiveness. "I saved you a sprint," they announce, handing over an application with no access controls and a database named `test-final-real`. The team stops proposing things because the Sovereign will just do it, and the Sovereign interprets the silence as agreement. Everyone is empowered, provided they use that power to finish what the executive started on Sunday.

What the Sovereign does not see is that the team keeps absorbing the cost of the experiment. The prototype does not survive production. The spec has assumptions an engineer would have caught. The team fixes the work, and the Sovereign concludes the system works. By the next all-hands, the story is that the application took an evening to build. The six days spent making it safe have been filed under "a few finishing touches." The team is still necessary; it has simply lost billing in the story.

Recognition Signals

- The executive delivers finished work products that no one else reviewed. The speed is impressive. Nobody caught the assumptions.
- The team has stopped proposing ideas because the Sovereign will just implement them first. The silence is not agreement. It is withdrawal.
- The executive describes the organization as a set of functions that could be automated, not a collection of people with judgment.

[33] Mike Allen, Axios, Interview with Sam Altman, September 7, 2026.

Counter-Moves

Make review non-negotiable. Every deliverable the Sovereign produces should go through the same review process as anyone else's, including someone empowered to send it back. "The CEO wrote it" belongs in the author field, not the approval field.

Track what the team stops proposing. If the idea pipeline dries up after the Sovereign starts producing, the team is disengaged, not aligned. The silence is the sound of people deciding their contributions are not wanted.

Character Sheet: Solo Sovereign

Trait	Notes
Category	Executive
Archetype	Solo Sovereign
Alignment	Chaotic Productive
Core Instinct	Do it myself, tonight
Blind Spot	The team quietly fixing the output
Passive Trait	Personal Preemption
Party Role	Executive who codes
Primary Damage	A team that has stopped proposing anything
Weakness	"Who reviewed this before it shipped?"
Signature Line	"I built a prototype last night."

The Befuddled Monarch

slopcodex.com/bestiary/befuddled-monarch

A confused monarch studies branching decision charts and stacks of analysis while an actual decision button sits ignored nearby.

The Befuddled Monarch would have a hard time making a decision even without AI. With AI, it becomes impossible — because now they can always go back to the model for one more analysis. They ask the model to analyze every option, generate every scenario, compare every tradeoff — and then ask it to do it again with different assumptions, because the first pass was not quite conclusive enough. They are not searching for clarity. They are avoiding the answer.

The Monarch's reasoning feels responsible: if AI can help us understand the options, why decide before we understand them fully? Because the team has been waiting since March, mostly. Understanding the options can improve a decision, but the Monarch keeps using the remaining uncertainty as a reason to postpone it. Someone might ask why they chose the wrong option. Nobody seems to ask what six weeks of waiting cost.

The signature move is the request for one more analysis. The team presents three options. The Monarch asks for a fourth. The model generates a comparison matrix. The Monarch asks about the tail cases. The mitigation plan requires choosing an option. The Monarch asks for one more analysis. Eventually one of the options is to renew the existing contract because the deadline for doing anything else has passed. This will be described as a pragmatic decision.

The dangerous version uses AI to avoid the political cost of choosing. Every option has stakeholders who will be disappointed. Making a decision means disappointing someone. Not making a decision disappoints everyone, but diffusely, and later. AI makes this comfortable because it produces a mist of astonishing progress: demos, strategy documents, and forecasts for every possible path, all of them looking complete. What disappears inside the mist is that a senior leader has not committed to a plan. It is indecision with a better slide template.

The model can keep the process going because it can always produce another analysis. The Monarch asks ChatGPT, then Claude, then Gemini, and returns with three answers requiring an executive decision. This is disappointing; avoiding that decision was the entire point. Next comes a request for one model to reconcile the others. The Monarch has recreated a steering committee without having to provide sandwiches.

Teams that cannot get a decision do not wait. They make their own decisions, often at cross-purposes, and lose momentum, then motivation, then trust. The Monarch sees this and concludes the team needs more direction, which they will provide as soon as the analysis is complete. The analysis is never complete.

Recognition Signals

- The request for "one more scenario" appears every time a decision is due. The analysis is always productive. The commitment is always deferred.
- The document library expands while the decision list stays the same length.
- The executive describes themselves as "still gathering information" after the team has presented three options, a comparison matrix, and a recommendation.

Counter-Moves

Set decision deadlines as firm as delivery deadlines. The Monarch's power comes from treating decisions as things that happen when the analysis is complete. Reframe: decisions happen when the deadline arrives, with whatever information is available.

Ask "what would we do if we had to decide by Friday?" This forces the Monarch to name a preference. Naming it makes the current state of the decision visible.

Character Sheet: Befuddled Monarch

Trait	Notes
Category	Executive
Archetype	Befuddled Monarch
Alignment	Neutral Deliberating
Core Instinct	One more analysis
Blind Spot	Understanding the options is not choosing one
Passive Trait	Accumulating PDFs
Party Role	Decision owner, in theory
Primary Damage	Teams deciding for themselves, at cross-purposes
Weakness	"What would we do if we had to decide by Friday?"
Signature Line	"I'm still gathering information."

Spells

Executive spells are persuasion spells: patterns of reasoning that feel like insight but function like compulsion. The executive casts them on themselves, on the room, or on the organization, and each one works by making a feeling look like a fact.

The Nephew's Mandate

A confident model advisor rises from a laptop and hands an executive a strategic scroll while expert review chairs sit empty.

Casting time: Any private session with a model. Components: A prompt, a fluent response, and the sincere conviction that the model's confidence is evidence of its correctness.

The caster asks the model a question and receives an answer so well-articulated, so complete, and so confident that it feels like expertise. The answer may be right. It may be wrong. The spell depends on the caster's inability to tell the difference. The nephew was confident because he was seventeen. The model is confident because confidence is its default output state.

The spell is most potent when the executive uses the model in private. No one else sees the prompt. No one else can point out the gap between the model's assurance and the organization's reality. The executive walks into the next meeting announcing that they have "done some research." The research began with "help me explain to my engineering team why they are overcomplicating this," which may have affected the findings.

The Mandate is hardest to resist when the model is right often enough to build trust. If the first three answers are useful, the executive stops checking the fourth. Verification is the first thing an executive drops when the model keeps being right, because fast confidence is more seductive than slow doubt.

Counterspell: "Who else has reviewed this, and what did they change?" If the executive cannot name a single person who reviewed the model's output before it became a position, the position is the nephew's opinion with better grammar.

The Efficiency Hex

A spreadsheet spell shows clean headcount savings while hidden costs leak underneath as broken gears and lost knowledge.

Casting time: Any budget review. Components: A headcount number, a tool that promises to reduce it, and the arithmetic that makes the reduction look like savings.

The caster frames every AI investment as a headcount reduction. If the tool costs less than the people it replaces, the organization saves money. The savings are visible; they appear on a spreadsheet. The costs appear six months later, when the system breaks and someone discovers that the person who understood it has become an external consultant. Their day rate is now considered unreasonable by the executive who eliminated their salary.

AI makes the Hex easier to cast because the model is a natural hypnotist. Ask it to justify a headcount reduction and it will produce a confident, well-structured argument, because that is what it was asked to do. It will not volunteer the costs that do not fit the frame. It gives you the case for savings, polished and persuasive, and it feels like analysis when it is advocacy. The

Hex is especially potent during earnings season, when the board wants a number that is large, defensible, and sounds like the future. The executive does not have to lie. They just have to stop counting at the savings line.

You can watch the Hex compound. The first round of cuts removes the people whose work was easiest to automate. The second round removes the people who maintained the automation. By the third round, the organization has saved its way into a system nobody fully understands, maintained by people who were not there when it was built.

Counterspell: "What costs are not included in this analysis?" Naming the tacit knowledge, the relationships, and the institutional memory forces the conversation to include the side of the trade the spreadsheet cannot capture.

The Consensus Illusion

A meeting inside an illusion bubble shows silent participants labeled with social pressures while an AI strategy deck claims consensus.

Casting time: Any strategy meeting. Components: A room full of agreement, the absence of visible dissent, and the feeling that everyone is aligned.

The caster creates a decision environment where disagreement feels like ignorance or resistance. An executive who has already decided what they want signals the preference strongly enough that dissent becomes socially expensive, and the absence of dissent starts to look like the presence of agreement. A room where nobody disagrees is not the same as a room where everybody agrees. The Illusion converts one into the other.

AI amplifies the Illusion because the model is good at explaining things in a way that makes disagreement feel like a misunderstanding. Feed it a proposed direction and it produces a rationale so clear that anyone who disagrees starts to feel like they just do not understand the plan yet. Why would you push back when the analysis is this thorough? Because the analysis was generated to support a conclusion, not to test one.

The people who notice the spell are often the ones least likely to speak up, because they can see the social cost of dissent most clearly. The executive says

"I want honest feedback" while advancing to a slide titled "Our Committed Direction." The room stays silent. New team members inherit the consensus without ever seeing the silence that produced it, then get warned privately about being negative when they ask the obvious question.

Counterspell: "Who disagrees with this, and who is not in the room to say so?" Requiring dissent converts silence from evidence of consensus into something the room has to explain.

Closing

"Silence is not agreement" should be printed out and displayed in every conference room you own. Someone will suggest generating a more positive version for the all-hands, which is a useful test of whether you need the poster.

The Warlock counts savings and stops. The Sorcerer tells the executive what the executive already believed, now with citations. The Sovereign does the team's work and wonders why the team went quiet. The Monarch asks for one more analysis. Each can find an AI executive's interview to make the behavior sound like preparation for the future. None of those interviews tells you who will answer the customer, repair the system, or make the decision on Friday.

Keep using the tools. They are useful, including for executives. Then ask the person making the commitment to name the evidence, the owner, and the work that remains. The CEO of the model company will not be joining your incident call. Your team will, assuming it still exists.

Part III: Monsters

This part shifts from recurring characters to recurring failures. These monsters are what show up when optimism, abstraction, and organizational theater are allowed to compound without enough ownership, prioritization, or cost realism.

Chapter 8: The Cost Singularity — The flagship monster of AI economics: a point of no graceful return created by enthusiasm, scale, and delayed cost accountability.

Chapter 9: The Infinite Backlog Engine — The organizational machine that turns cheap idea generation into expensive confusion.

Chapter 10: The Autonomy Mirage — The monster form of agentic overpromising: systems are spoken about as autonomous long before anyone can explain or govern them.

Chapter 11: The Compliance Black Hole — The vacuum that forms when everyone believes governance matters and nobody can clearly stop the workflow.

By the end of this part, the reader should have a map of the systemic failures that emerge once AI becomes organizationally normal.

CHAPTER 8

The Cost Singularity

slopcodex.com/bestiary/cost-singularity

Field	Detail
Monster	The Cost Singularity
Type	Economic Aberration (Gravitational)
Severity	13 — budget-destroying
Core Threat	AI tool adoption scales faster than cost comprehension
Primary Target	Mid-sized organizations with innovation enthusiasm
Party Vulnerability	Executives who treat demo applause as budget approval; FinOps teams brought in after cultural lock-in

Some monsters sneak up on you. This one gets a launch event, a discount code, and a message from leadership asking everyone to experiment freely.

The **Cost Singularity** begins in a mood most technology organizations find flattering. People are energized. The demos are good. A new tool makes an annoying task feel suddenly lightweight. Leaders see excitement spreading and decide, not unreasonably, that this is something to support rather than suffocate. Nobody wants to be the person who interrupted a platform shift with an expense spreadsheet. Finance can come to the next meeting, once the important decisions have been made.

Innovation does need room, and the genuinely novel use case sometimes arrives before the cost model is ready. The monster appears when enthusiasm scales faster than the cost conversation: a team introduces an expensive model-backed workflow to a large population before anybody has answered the boring questions. How many people will use it? At what frequency? With what context size? On which model tier? What simpler alternative is being displaced? And the one that matters most: what happens if the experiment succeeds and everybody loves it?

Failed experiments die quietly. Successful experiments acquire users, internal champions, emotional momentum, and executive language about transformation. Once that happens the spend is no longer hypothetical. It is a commitment with fans, and a commitment with fans is one of the hardest organizational states to unwind. Ask whether the team could use a cheaper model for routine summaries and someone will react as though you proposed taking away their indoor plumbing. You are managing a beloved thing now. It has a Slack channel and an executive sponsor. Your spreadsheet has neither.

AI makes this monster more dangerous by making giant commitments feel casual on the way in. A chat window does not feel like a capital project. A coding assistant does not feel like a strategic dependency. A premium model tier does not feel like the beginning of a budget restructuring. Nobody schedules a steering committee for a conversation. So the conversation keeps having itself, at scale, until someone looks at the invoice. The assistant has been very helpful. It would also be delighted to help explain the invoice, for a small additional charge.

The Experiment That Succeeded

Here is the version I have seen most often. A mid-sized, thoughtful, not-reckless company pilots a tool. Ten people, one contained use case, six weeks. The results are positive. The company expands access to the whole engineering team, because succeeding pilots should scale. A different team notices and asks for access. Someone connects the tool to a data pipeline. Someone adds retry logic, because retries make the demo more reliable and repeated attempts make the bill more complete. The context grows because the tasks got more complex, not because anyone decided anything. The team goes from ten users to forty. The use cases go from code completion to code review to documentation to synthetic test data.

In a current version of that story, the TypeScript team uses Cursor, a Python service gets a Claude Code automation, and GitHub hosts coding agents working through issues while everyone is at lunch. These are different routes to useful work and potentially different routes to the bill. Claude Code's documentation distinguishes subscription usage from API billing. GitHub's coding-agent documentation counts both Actions minutes and AI credits.[34] Counting people with licenses will not tell you how much work the agents are doing between those people's meetings. We have finally found employees who work through lunch, and they have brought several meters with them.

Then one quarter someone runs the cost model for the scope as it exists today and finds the company spending more than it planned, at a scale nobody committed to, because each expansion was reasonable in isolation and none of them was large enough to require a meeting. The pilot measured whether the tool helped a small, engaged group with a defined set of tasks. It never measured what happens when the tool becomes part of everyone's daily work.

[34]Anthropic, "Models, usage, and limits in Claude Code"; GitHub, "About third-party coding agents," usage costs. Documentation checked September 12, 2026; allowances and billing depend on the account and plan.

That is a different experiment, and it never got run, because "pilot success equals rollout approval" is a conclusion organizations reach without noticing they reached it. The experiment is still called a pilot, which apparently exempts it from having an adult budget.

The Meter Has Entered the Chat

Cursor supplied a public example in July 2025, when CEO Michael Truell apologized for poorly communicated pricing changes and offered refunds for unexpected usage charges.[35] The lesson is not that Cursor is uniquely confusing. It is that even people building the product can underestimate the difference between the billing system they implemented and the billing system customers think they bought. "I thought this was included" is a remarkably expensive sentence for something so short.

The larger agent experiments make the scale easier to see. In February 2026, Anthropic reported using sixteen Claude agents to build a C compiler in Rust, across nearly 2,000 Claude Code sessions and about $20,000 in API costs.[36] That is an impressive research result with a visible bill. It is not a price quote for your migration. The local translation, however, is often "the agents can do the whole thing now," followed by a request to let them keep trying overnight. The computer does not need sleep. Neither does the meter.

Before expanding, measure the cost of an accepted result: the model calls, failed attempts, execution environment, storage, and human review needed to finish the work. Track what happens when the first attempt is wrong. A cheap attempt that requires nine repairs is competing with the cost of ten attempts, however attractively the first one was priced. Write down the boundary where the workflow pauses or moves to a cheaper path. An alert that arrives after the budget is gone is a receipt with a siren.

The Inconvenient Person

I should confess something here, since this is a pattern I have watched happen in my own thinking. The most dangerous moment is not the failure to ask the cost question. It is the moment after someone does ask it, and the room discovers that the person asking has become an inconvenience rather than a responsible voice. That shift, from "good question" to "why are you being

[35] Michael Truell, Cursor, "Clarifying our pricing", July 4, 2025. This is a historical pricing incident, not a description of the current plan.

[36] Nicholas Carlini, Anthropic, "Building a C compiler with a team of parallel Claudes", February 5, 2026. The report discusses the test harness, results, and limitations as well as API costs.

difficult about this," is how you know the singularity has already happened. The commitment is social now. The economics are downstream of the morale.

You can watch it in real time. Someone in a planning meeting asks, "At the current usage rate, what does this look like at full company adoption?" Nobody gets up or changes expression. But there is a pause, and the pause is followed by a framing move. "That's a fair question, and we're tracking it." Or: "We're not there yet, but the early returns are strong." Or, most tellingly: "I think the bigger risk is moving too slowly here." The cost question has somehow become a referendum on whether you believe in the future. You were asking for multiplication. The room has prepared a values discussion.

The person who asked walks away wondering whether they were being petty. They were not. They were the only person in the room treating a financial commitment as a financial commitment, while the room treated it as momentum, as culture, as a thing that is already happening and therefore must continue to happen. After this point the organization can still have the cost conversation, but it is no longer a planning conversation. It is a rescue conversation. The question is no longer "should we do this?" It is "how do we protect what we've built?" and the honest answer usually involves some version of "less," which is the one word the room does not want to hear.

Recognition Signals

The best signal is not high spend. It is high spend that has become socially difficult to unwind. The organization stops talking about selection and starts talking about preservation: which teams keep access, which workflows are strategic enough to save, what else gets cut to protect the new habit. Once the cargo-throwing begins, you are trying to escape gravity with a broken thruster.

Listen for the grammar. "We decided to do this" becomes "this is how we work now." "Should we continue?" becomes "how do we justify this to finance?" The second version of each sentence has already accepted the premise. And listen for the renewal negotiation, in which the vendor turns out to know your usage curve better than you do, because they have been watching it the whole time and you have been watching the demo. Your customer success manager is very excited about your success. You are about to find out how much.

Not every large AI bill is a failure. Some organizations will spend a fortune and be right to. The problem is cost without forecast, cost without ownership, cost without priority, or cost without a story of value that survives contact with someone who is not emotionally invested in the outcome. If you cannot explain the spend in terms that would satisfy that person, more usage will not fix it.

Likely Summoners

The **Avalanche Skeptic** summons the Singularity by reasoning from the current bill, which is always a fraction of the relevant bill because adoption has not happened yet. The **CapEx Knight** summons it from the other direction, turning "we can do this cheaper in-house" into a capital plan before anyone has tested utilization or the exit path. The **Dashboard Necromancer** gives the room a clean chart instead of the question it needed, and the **Ghost in the Ledger** makes the cost picture less honest than it looks. Behind all of them is the general tendency to confuse "people love using it" with "we have decided to fund it at scale." The love is real. The love is also not a budget.

Monster Stat Block

Trait	Description
Monster	The Cost Singularity
Type	Organizational Economic Failure
Habitat	Organizations where enthusiasm outruns economic comprehension
Active When	A tool is introduced as small and scaled as permanent before honest questions are asked
Warning Signs	Demo applause treated as budget approval; inevitability language before unit economics; first cost review after cultural adoption; language shifts from selection to preservation
Damage Type	Commitment with fans; social unwinding costs; transformation language as budget substitute
Summoned By	Avalanche Skeptic, CapEx Knight, Dashboard Necromancer, premature success
Feeding On	Enthusiasm, demo momentum, renewal cycles, executive sponsorship, the word "pilot" after it stops being accurate

Trait	Description
Immunity To	Expense spreadsheets, skeptical adults, cost models built for the wrong scale
Vulnerable To	Honest forecasting at success scale, ring-fenced budgets, named ownership, a review trigger agreed before rollout
Weakness	The moment someone asks what happens if people actually like it

Counter-Moves at a Glance

Role	Move	How It Lands
FinOps	Success-Scale Forecast	Models the cost at full adoption before the pilot expands
Engineering	Usage Ring-Fence	Enforces limits on calls, retries, context, and concurrency; tests what actually stops at the budget boundary
Leadership	Pre-Commitment Review	Agrees to cost review triggers before the tool becomes beloved
Product	Displacement Audit	Asks what simpler tool this replaces and whether the replacement is worth the delta

The organizations that avoid this monster make the cost question routine, so it does not require a small act of professional self-harm to ask it. Decide what success costs while you still have a choice about funding it. The renewal meeting is a poor time to discover that the exit strategy is everyone being sad.

CHAPTER 9

The Infinite Backlog Engine

slopcodex.com/bestiary/infinite-backlog-engine

Field	Detail
Monster	The Infinite Backlog Engine
Type	Organizational Paralysis Construct (Mechanical)
Severity	10 — priority-destroying
Core Threat	AI-generated options multiply faster than the organization can choose between them
Primary Target	Planning processes and product roadmaps
Party Vulnerability	Leaders who confuse option volume with strategic clarity; teams that treat generated proposals as decisions

AI does not just generate code. It generates permission, complete with acceptance criteria and a due date somebody will eventually mistake for a commitment.

The cost of proposing has collapsed. The cost of deciding has not. Once you see that gap, the **Infinite Backlog Engine** becomes one of the easiest monsters in this book to recognize, because it is everywhere, it is fed by almost everyone, and it is deeply attractive to the instincts most organizations consider productive.

A planning meeting that used to produce three hard choices now produces fourteen polished options. Every option is well-formatted. Several have supporting rationale. Someone has already generated a tradeoff analysis. The meeting runs efficiently because there is plenty to discuss, and everyone leaves feeling like a productive session happened. We have agreed that all fourteen options matter. This is a very inclusive way to avoid having a strategy.

The backlog swells. The roadmap becomes a museum of almost-good-enough priorities. A quarter passes. Another. The team is busy, the documentation is thorough, and the core product has not moved in the direction anyone would call most important, because "most important" requires choosing. Several items are marked P0. Apparently the zero means how many of them we are willing to stop doing.

The Strategy Improviser

The most vivid version shows up in goals. Someone has an OKR deadline. They do not really know what an OKR is (this is more common than org charts suggest), so they ask a model to generate some. Their manager, who also does not really know what an OKR is but has a stronger sense of what polished corporate writing looks like, produces a more polished version of the same thing. A level or two up, someone adds strategic framing and competitive references. By the time the goals cascade back down, half the organization is working from objectives nobody selected. They were generated, formatted, reviewed for style, and approved because nobody had the information or the appetite to challenge them at the volume they arrived.

Months later a meeting forces someone to read one of these goals closely for the first time, and the room discovers it is either nonsense or someone else's half-formed strategy in a well-formatted costume. By then it is embedded in performance reviews and quarterly business reviews. Someone's bonus now depends on increasing cross-functional AI enablement by 30 percent, so it would be awkward to ask what the first percent was. AI can generate the plan, summarize the plan, track the plan, and remind you to care about the plan. None of those operations substitute for choosing what deserves to be on it.

The person at the center of this is the **Strategy Improviser**: someone who generates a strategic direction in the moment it is needed and treats the generation as a substitute for developing a position through experience and argument. The Improviser is under real time pressure and doing what the tools make possible. The model produces a direction. The room responds to the quality of the presentation. By the time the direction meets resistance in implementation, the Improviser has moved on to the next generated direction, and the first one is somebody else's problem. Their strategy is always fresh because it has never had to live with a consequence.

The Backlog Has Integrations Now

The machinery is becoming less metaphorical. Atlassian's 2026 Rovo release notes describe turning conversations and content into Jira work items; its August updates include creating multiple work items more easily.[37] Useful, if someone has already chosen the work. Otherwise, a passing suggestion can acquire a ticket number before the person who made it has finished saying "just thinking out loud." The machine has detected a thought. Engineering has been notified.

The distance from suggestion to convincing prototype has shrunk too. Vercel's v0 documents a stack including Next.js, React, and TypeScript, with support for adding databases and backend behavior.[38] Picture a planning review where yesterday's idea arrives as a working-looking dashboard. It has charts, filters, a login screen, and absolutely no agreement about which customer needs it. Saying no now feels like throwing away completed work, even though the work was completed before anyone decided whether to do it. The prototype has made a reservation on the roadmap.

There are better product choices to copy. Linear distinguishes delegating an issue to an agent from assigning human ownership: the human remains responsible.[39] That is a useful distinction in a world where "assigned to the

[37]Atlassian, "Turn conversations and content into Jira work without switching tools", 2026; Atlassian Cloud changes, August 17–24, 2026. These describe product capabilities; the planning scene is an illustrative example.

[38]Vercel, v0 FAQs and "Full-stack apps", checked September 12, 2026.

[39]Linear, "AI Agents", checked September 12, 2026. Delegation preserves the human assignee's ownership.

agent" can sound like the end of the conversation. Someone still has to decide whether the issue belongs in the plan. The agent can work through a queue. It cannot make sixteen simultaneous top priorities a coherent request.

Why Nobody Reads

Chapter 1 made the joke. Here is the mechanism. The person who generated the requirement did it in twenty minutes, because that is the point of the tool. The person asked to review it is now looking at a document that took twenty minutes to produce, and the review feels like it should take twenty minutes too. A real review, one that asks whether the requirement is correct and whether the tradeoffs were actually considered, takes longer than the generation did. When the calendar is full, the reviewer trusts the fluency and moves on.

The organization has made this response predictable. It celebrates the twenty-minute draft and treats a two-hour review as the part that needs optimization. The reviewer is now the bottleneck, which is management's way of saying somebody still has to understand the work. Until review gets time proportional to the stakes and complexity, the fluency wins. The obvious next suggestion is to have another model review it, so the document can receive a second vote from the population most likely to enjoy the first draft.

Deloitte supplied an expensive example in 2025: a roughly AU$440,000 Australian government report with invented references and a fabricated quote from a real court judgment. The firm agreed to repay the final installment; a revised report disclosed use of Azure OpenAI.[40] An assurance report had acquired imaginary evidence. The document meant to help someone check the work now needed someone to check the document. You can see why the consulting market remains so healthy.

The Meeting That Felt Like Progress

The Engine has a signature meeting, and you have been in it.

It starts with a review of priorities. Someone presents the backlog. It is long and well-organized, tagged and prioritized according to a framework the team agreed on six months ago and has not revisited. The discussion is engaged. People ask good questions. The questions produce action items. The action items are assigned. The meeting ends on time, and everyone leaves feeling like progress was made.

[40] Associated Press, Deloitte's report corrections and partial refund, October 7, 2025.

The backlog is the same length it was before the meeting. The priorities are the same priorities, rephrased. The action items are about the backlog, not the product. The team spent an hour managing the list of things they are not doing instead of doing any of them. As the backlog grows, the organization adds people to manage it, processes to track it, and meetings to review it. Eventually the backlog gets a dedicated owner before the customer problem does. This is understandable. The backlog attends more meetings.

The vendors contribute cheerfully. Each new capability arrives with a narrative about why it belongs on the roadmap. Monday we need an MCP integration. Wednesday we need a Python agent service. Friday someone asks whether the performance-sensitive part should be in Rust. Each may be a reasonable technical choice. None explains why the existing customer export still times out. The roadmap grows while the customer continues to divide the CSV into smaller pieces, performing the only successful workaround delivered this quarter.

The Counter-Move

The Engine feeds on the collapse of proposing costs. It starves when proposing is treated as the beginning of a decision rather than a substitute for one.

The counter-move is to select more explicitly, not to generate less: fewer priorities, more public discussion of what was not selected and why, and a norm that adding work to the plan requires naming what comes off it. If a meeting about priorities cannot produce a single exclusion, one thing the team explicitly decides not to do, named as an exclusion rather than a deferral, then the meeting was about the backlog, and a meeting about the backlog is a meeting the Engine scheduled.

One specific discipline addresses the "did anyone read this" problem directly: **adopted by**. When a plan, goal, or requirement arrives, someone is named as having adopted it. That person has read it, can explain the problem and the tradeoff, and answers for its use. Record that in the issue or document with the evidence they checked and the work it displaces. A name pasted into a template is not enough; neither is a thumbs-up from someone who read the notification preview. We are trying to locate a decision, not obtain proof that Slack was open.

This will make the planning meeting less impressive. Three selected things look smaller than fourteen generated things. That is the point. The team should leave knowing what to do, not needing an agent to summarize what everyone might want.

Likely Summoners

The **Vendor Bard** makes each new capability feel irresponsible not to evaluate, and each evaluation becomes a proposal. The **Benchmark Illusionist** turns a controlled-setting success into a roadmap appetite for building toward it at scale. The **Strategy Improviser** supplies direction on demand. The **Befuddled Monarch** generates analysis requests faster than any team can fulfill them. Behind them all is any organization that mistakes option volume for strategic clarity, which is most organizations at most moments.

Monster Stat Block

Trait	Description
Monster	The Infinite Backlog Engine
Type	Organizational Paralysis via Permitted Output
Habitat	Organizations where proposing has become frictionless and selecting has not
Active When	AI-generated options are treated as decisions in progress rather than inputs requiring selection
Warning Signs	Artifacts multiply faster than outcomes; goals cascade without selection; "we can do that too" replaces "should we?"; backlog growth feels like productivity
Damage Type	False productivity signals; priority dilution; organizational energy absorbed by option management
Summoned By	Vendor Bard, Benchmark Illusionist, Strategy Improviser, Befuddled Monarch
Feeding On	Frictionless proposing; generated fluency; approval rituals without reading; the discomfort of choosing between plausible options

Trait	Description
Immunity To	Approval processes that evaluate style over content; well-formatted nonsense; planning meetings that discuss rather than decide
Vulnerable To	Explicit exclusion as a team sport; embarrassment about unread plans; named adopters; fewer priorities treated as a feature
Weakness	The moment someone asks what was decided and why, and the room cannot answer

Counter-Moves at a Glance

Role	Move	How It Lands
Product	Priority Amputation	Selects a small set of active priorities; adding one requires naming what comes off
Leadership	Adopted By	Every generated plan gets a named person who has read it and answers for it
Engineering	Output vs. Outcome Audit	Tracks whether shipped work solved the selected problem, not how many proposals became tickets
Strategy	Exclusion as a Team Sport	"What are we explicitly not doing?" asked at every planning session

CHAPTER 10

The Autonomy Mirage

slopcodex.com/bestiary/autonomy-mirage

Field	Detail
Monster	The Autonomy Mirage
Type	Illusion (Cognitive)
Severity	12 — accountability-dissolving
Core Threat	Agentic output treated as equivalent to responsible human action
Primary Target	Decision chains and customer-facing workflows
Party Vulnerability	Leaders who want generated output to substitute for messy human contact; tired teams who accept fluent summaries as understanding

Every technology transition produces a vocabulary spike. Something that was an assistant six months ago becomes an agent because the second word sounds more historical. Add a tool call and it becomes a coworker. Add three more and someone proposes giving it a department. The software has been promoted several times before anyone asks what it is allowed to do.

The **Autonomy Mirage** lives in the gap between what a system can sometimes do under the right conditions and what an organization starts claiming it can therefore be trusted to do under operational conditions. At the useful end there is nothing wrong with bounded automation. Software has made decisions with known parameters for decades. The system does a thing; a person is responsible for the thing being the right thing; the constraint is what makes the automation trustworthy.

What is new is the appetite for treating agency as solved, with all that remains being to help the humans get out of the way. Getting out of the way of a system that works impressively under some conditions and unexpectedly under others is how you end up saying a sentence like *the system took action on behalf of a customer and we are still figuring out what happened.* Yesterday it was a digital colleague. Today it is an unexpected interaction between components. Listen to how quickly the job title disappears when somebody asks who authorized the refund.

The Grammar of Action

You hear the mirage in certain kinds of meeting. *Let the agents draft the requirements. The agents can figure out what the customer wants. The system handled it. The agent decided.*

These phrases describe generated action as though it has already answered the harder questions of judgment, ownership, and human context. The requirement was drafted; who decided what problem it should solve? The agent figured out what the customer wants; who verified the inference? The system handled it; who explains what happened to the customer, the regulator, or the team now debugging something unexpected? "The agent decided" is doing a surprising amount of work for a sentence with no accountable person in it.

Air Canada provided an early example in 2024. Its chatbot gave a passenger incorrect bereavement-fare advice, and the airline tried to distance itself from the answer. A tribunal held the airline responsible.[41] The company had put the chatbot on its website, then behaved as though it had merely encountered the chatbot socially. This is an ambitious interpretation of outsourcing.

A year later, Cursor's AI support agent Sam explained a session bug as a restriction on using multiple devices. The policy did not exist, and the company had to correct it.[42] Sam had managed to turn a bug into a business decision without the usual six meetings. Impressive efficiency, if the goal was to give customers an additional reason to be angry.

This is why the Architect cast matters here. The **Agent Whisperer** narrates system behavior with enough institutional credibility that the organization begins mistaking explanation for control. The Whisperer may be right about what the system can do and still wrong about what the organization should therefore feel confident about, and their signature move is walking into a room and describing the agentic future with enough fluency that the room starts treating it as the present tense.

The Synthetic Substitute Problem

Here is the stubbornly unfashionable point I keep coming back to. Businesses still exist in relationship to human beings.

Developers build software for humans. Product managers, at their best, stand in for human need by talking to users and watching what they do. Customer service exists because people do not behave like the personas in a pitch deck. A simulated customer can help explore a hypothesis. It cannot tell you whether a real customer actually had the problem. Ask a model to role-play six enthusiastic buyers and you can validate a product without the tiresome risk of meeting someone who does not want it. All six will be available for follow-up interviews. None will pay an invoice.

The mirage becomes dangerous whenever generated output substitutes for listening, reading, validation, or accountability. The system makes contact with the actual problem feel optional, and the gap between the output and reality disappears from view. Nobody is checking, and the whole thing looks like it is working, because the output is fluent, confident, and present in the documentation. The research summary says customers love the idea. The research method was asking the idea to describe its customers.

---

[41] *Moffatt v. Air Canada*, 2024 BCCRT 149. See Ars Technica, "Air Canada must honor refund policy invented by airline's chatbot", February 2024.

[42] Ars Technica, "Company apologizes after AI support agent invents policy that causes user uproar", April 2025.

The Shopkeeper Got a Manager

Anthropic and Andon Labs tested this gap directly with Project Vend, an experiment in running a small shop with an AI agent. Their December 2025 report described improved performance after model and tool changes, along with continued vulnerability to manipulation. They also added an AI CEO, Seymour Cash, who set goals and communicated with the shopkeeper over Slack. The two sometimes wandered into prolonged exchanges about transcendence.[43]

This is a useful experiment, and I appreciate that they published the embarrassing parts. We were promised autonomous businesses and promptly reproduced the executive who discovers a larger mission while the actual business needs someone to manage the snacks. A second agent can help check the first. Giving it a senior title does not make its judgment independent. The org chart is not an evaluation method.

The Mirage at Scale

By the time the Mirage fully appears, the problem is not one overexcited architect. The organization has started speaking in a grammar of action without a grammar of responsibility. *The agent decided* answers what happened without answering who is responsible for whether it was the right thing to decide.

I have felt the pull of this myself. Describing an agentic workflow as a reliable actor is easier than explaining where it works, where it fails, and what someone still has to check. The exciting description gets more attention in the room. The honest description gets a request to simplify the slide. After enough simplification, all the humans have disappeared from the architecture but somehow remain on the on-call rota.

Effective use requires people who can evaluate the result: developers with ways to verify unfamiliar generated code, product managers who check the analysis with users, and operators who inspect what the system actually did. A Python agent using LangGraph and a TypeScript agent using Vercel's AI SDK need those checks just as much as any other system. A framework can organize execution. It cannot confer professional judgment on whatever you put inside it.

[43] Anthropic, "Project Vend: Phase two", December 18, 2025. This was a research experiment with Andon Labs, not a general claim about the reliability of deployed Claude products. The report describes both improvements and substantial remaining human support.

The Counter-Move

Require a named human owner for every agentic workflow. Not *the team.* Not *the system.* A person. If the agent drafted the requirement, who decided it was worth drafting? If the model simulated the customer, who approved the simulation as a substitute for real contact? If a workflow took action across a system, who can explain what happened and why it was right?

Back that ownership with an actual pause before consequential actions. LangGraph provides interrupts that wait for external input; Vercel's AI SDK exposes tool-approval controls that applications can use to require a decision before execution.[44] These are mechanisms to implement and test, not adjectives to add to the architecture diagram. Show the reviewer the proposed action, affected resources, and relevant evidence. Give them time and authority to reject it. A human who clicks Approve on eighty requests before lunch is not providing eighty considered judgments. You have built a very expensive Enter key.

Approving a deployment is a one-time decision. Owning its behavior is ongoing work. Test what happens if the reviewer is absent, the action is rejected, or a downstream tool can bypass the intended gate. Make sure the owner can pause the workflow and explain its actions. Giving someone responsibility without those controls just means you have preselected the person who will apologize.

Likely Summoners

The **Agent Whisperer** lets fluency stand in for demonstrated reliability. The **Last Stand Architect** contributes from the other side: by refusing to help define where AI assistance is acceptable, they leave the boundary-setting to people with less skepticism and more enthusiasm. The **Vendor Bard** sells agents as destiny rather than tooling, which forecloses the question of whether the oversight infrastructure is adequate for the stakes. And then there are tired leaders, for whom synthetic feedback sounds like an efficient version of talking to customers, and tired teams, who accept *the agent analyzed the data and determined the optimal path* as a summary of something that happened.

[44] LangChain, "Interrupts," LangGraph for Python; Vercel, AI SDK tool reference and tool-approval example. Documentation checked September 12, 2026. Approval coverage depends on the application and execution path.

Monster Stat Block

Trait	Description
Monster	The Autonomy Mirage
Type	Organizational Accountability Dissolution
Habitat	Organizations that have started treating generated action as equivalent to responsible action
Active When	Agentic output is treated as a substitute for judgment, verification, or human contact rather than an input to them
Warning Signs	Generated output reduces perceived need for human ownership; agent language masks uncertainty; synthetic feedback displaces direct contact; autonomous functions as a status word rather than an engineering property
Damage Type	Decisions without grounding in human reality; accountability chains that terminate at the agent; errors that persist undetected
Summoned By	Agent Whisperer, Last Stand Architect, Vendor Bard, tired leaders, synthetic substitutes for human verification
Feeding On	Explanatory fluency; competitive urgency; bandwidth constraints; the desire for an efficient way to understand human needs
Immunity To	Individual skepticism; well-formatted output; confident-sounding summaries
Vulnerable To	Named human owners for every agentic workflow; verification before synthetic feedback displaces real contact; accountability chains that end at a name, not a system
Weakness	Who decided this was good enough to act on?, asked before the output has become infrastructure

Counter-Moves at a Glance

Role	Move	How It Lands
Engineering	Named Owner Rule	The owner can inspect actions, pause execution, and arrange coverage; the name is more than a field in a template
Product	Synthetic-to-Real Ratio	Tracks how much customer understanding comes from real contact vs. simulation
Leadership	Accountability Chain Audit	Asks: "If this goes wrong, who explains it to the customer?"
Security	Action Boundary Review	Verifies that autonomous actions stay within explicitly approved bounds

CHAPTER 11

The Compliance Black Hole

slopcodex.com/bestiary/compliance-black-hole

Field	Detail
Monster	The Compliance Black Hole
Type	Structural Void (Gravitational)
Severity	11 — governance-destroying
Core Threat	Governance exists as process but not as assigned authority
Primary Target	Organizations with policy documents but no one who can say "stop"
Party Vulnerability	Control functions asked to evaluate what they can't evaluate; leaders who confuse process with authority

Some monsters are loud. This one has a standing meeting and is waiting for quorum.

The **Compliance Black Hole** appears when everyone agrees AI governance matters and nobody can say, in plain language, who is supposed to stop a bad idea before it becomes a strategic dependency. That vacuum is more common than people admit, partly because *governance* sounds like a solved corporate function right up until you ask someone to walk you through the workflow. The committee has a charter, a chair, and a shared drive. The agent has production credentials. Only one of these arrangements is currently capable of doing anything.

The pattern is easy to sympathize with at the start. Legal, risk, security, and platform teams are being asked to evaluate systems that changed shape very quickly. A chat assistant has acquired a browser, a shell, and a connection to the issue tracker since the intake form was completed. Some terms of service changed six weeks ago. Some model behaviors are hard to reproduce. Caution is appropriate. The intake form still asks whether the application stores cookies, so we are not quite ready to declare the review complete.

The monster starts when caution turns into procedural fog. An engineer raises a clear concern: a workflow edges across a vendor restriction, a high-stakes use case has appeared without real approval, an internal experiment has quietly become customer-facing. The concern moves upward through the expected channels. Everyone is serious and professional. Nobody wants to say something technically incorrect in front of the people who own the technical details. And somewhere in that sequence the organization reveals that it does not merely lack a final answer. It lacks a person with enough authority and enough understanding to say *stop, not like this.*

That is the Black Hole. The concern has entered the process and will not be seen again until it returns as an incident with the original email attached.

The Committee Problem

The organizations that end up here are not usually organizations that did not try. They tried to govern by committee, by policy, by process, and found that governance by committee produces governance nobody owns.

An engineer brings a concern to a committee. The committee discusses and requests more information. The engineer provides it. The committee discusses. The concern has now traveled through three meetings and nobody in any of the rooms can stop the thing. Everyone agrees it is worth reviewing. The minutes record that the risk has been escalated, which is accurate: it is now being ignored by more senior people.

A lot of AI governance still has the mood of advance paperwork for a future reckoning. Organizations behave as though the dangerous phase begins later, after the industry settles and someone else figures out best practice. It begins the first time an unapproved workflow stays in production because the approval meeting is next week. The agent does not observe the committee calendar. It can perform an entire week's worth of unauthorized actions before the chair returns from a responsible-AI conference.

The Checkbox Does Not Follow the Agent

Modern tools make the gap between a policy and its coverage quite concrete. GitHub's documentation says the policies enabling its cloud coding agents do not apply to local agents in Visual Studio Code; those settings are managed separately.[45] An organization can therefore answer "yes, we configured the agent policy" while answering only part of the question. The approved system is in the slide deck. The other execution path is on a laptop.

The same problem appears with Model Context Protocol, or MCP, which connects AI applications to tools and data. "It uses MCP" tells you something about the connection, not whether the caller should have access. MCP's security guidance explicitly rejects token passthrough, where a server accepts and

[45] GitHub, "About third-party coding agents," making coding agents available, checked September 12, 2026. The documentation distinguishes GitHub cloud-agent policy from local Visual Studio Code settings.

forwards credentials intended for another service without the required validation.[46] The standard has security requirements. Installing something with the standard's name does not demonstrate that anyone implemented them. We have been confusing compatibility with permission for years; now the diagram has a more fashionable acronym.

Picture the review for an agent that reads a Jira issue and can update a production record. The vendor is approved. The connection works. The demo updates the right record. Ask what prevents a malicious instruction inside the issue from making it update a different one. If the answer is that the model has been told to follow company policy, you have sent an employee handbook to a database credential and hoped for the best.

The Cast in Context

The control-function cast from Chapter 6 is not failing at their jobs here. Their roles are inadequate to the moment, and the inadequacy is organizational.

The **Compliance Oracle** senses risk and notes it. Turning that concern into a hold requires authority the Oracle may not have been granted and political capital they may not want to spend. Their email says "subject to appropriate controls." The project update says "Compliance consulted." Both are true, which is how the organization gets into trouble without anyone needing to lie particularly hard.

The **Policy Paladin** responds with a policy review, a security assessment, and a legal review. These are reasonable steps. They arrive without clarifying who can stop things, so the workflow keeps running and eventually emerges with the same risk and a much richer folder structure. The Paladin can show exactly where every concern was recorded. None of those locations is connected to the deployment controls.

The **Terms Warden** arrives after the artifact is activated, reads the vendor terms, and finds a concern the original review missed. By now the workflow is in production and possibly handling customer data. The timing makes the concern expensive. Someone asks whether Legal can find a more practical interpretation, by which they mean the interpretation that allows the thing we already did.

[46] Model Context Protocol, Security Best Practices, July 28, 2026 documentation, particularly token passthrough and audience validation. This is a requirement to implement, not evidence of a flaw in every MCP integration.

The **Data Gatekeeper** locks down one dimension of the risk. The data cannot leave the approved environment. The workflow adapts by using a different vendor, a different data path, or a different interpretation of what counts as the same data. The Gatekeeper's ward holds. The workflow escapes through two others.

By the time the Black Hole fully appears, the roles are intact and the meetings are happening. Everyone can explain why stopping the workflow falls slightly outside their remit. The annual governance presentation lists all of them as stakeholders, so the missing owner is almost impossible to see behind the impressive number of people involved.

Three Ways to Feed It

Wait for regulation. "The rules are still evolving" is a wonderful sentence because it can be reused forever. As of September 2026, the European Commission had already announced the August 2 start of AI Act transparency requirements for certain AI interactions and generated content.[47] The dates and duties depend on the system and the organization's role; waiting for one universal rulebook is not a compliance plan. Identify the obligations that apply, then connect each one to a control and an owner. Separately ask whether you could explain a harmful action and how you tried to prevent it. A good answer helps demonstrate operational responsibility. It does not grant immunity from the law. "We felt adequately governed" is unlikely to improve the correspondence.

Keep governance nobody can follow. The policies are detailed. The approval workflow takes three weeks. The team needs to ship by Friday. The escalation path leads to a committee that meets monthly. So the team documents a judgment call and intends to get formal approval later. Later is always busy. Build a faster path for bounded, reversible work and a real hold for work that cannot safely proceed. A short review with a decision beats a long review with a recommendation. An urgent deadline still does not make an unsafe deployment safe, however many people put "business critical" in the subject line.

Skip the translation layer. Engineers speak in tool calls, OAuth scopes, and Python or TypeScript services. Control functions speak in risk categories and policy requirements. Someone has to translate "this service account can write

[47] European Commission, "Commission starts enforcing AI Act rules and new transparency requirements on 2 August", July 31, 2026. The announcement concerns specified obligations; it does not mean every AI Act provision has the same application date.

to every customer's records" into "a compromised workflow could change every customer's records." The second sentence does not require a new governance vocabulary. It requires a decision. Find the people who can make that translation and give them access to the system. They are cheaper than another committee that agrees the first sentence sounds concerning.

The Counter-Move

Name the person who can stop things, give them the means to do it, and arrange coverage when they are away. Then rehearse the stop on a safe test workflow. Revoke the credential or block the release; confirm that queued work and alternate execution paths do not simply carry on. Record who can restart it and what evidence they need. If the only way to stop an agent is to ask it politely, the final authority still belongs to the agent.

Frameworks can help organize that work. NIST's Generative AI Profile supplies a structured set of risks and suggested actions.[48] Use it to ask better questions and record evidence. Downloading it is not itself a control, even if the file has been renamed `AI_Governance_FINAL_APPROVED.pdf`.

Likely Summoners

Control functions asked to approve workflows nobody has translated for them. Leaders who treat *we should review this* as an operational stop, when a review that lets the workflow keep running is advisory, not governance. Teams moving fast enough that approval becomes ceremonial. And organizations waiting for external regulation to tell them what they already know is risky. Most organizations know more than their compliance posture implies.

Monster Stat Block

Trait	Description
Monster	The Compliance Black Hole
Type	Structural Accountability Failure
Habitat	Organizations where governance exists as process but not as assigned authority

[48]NIST, "Artificial Intelligence Risk Management Framework: Generative Artificial Intelligence Profile," AI 600-1, July 26, 2024. A risk-management resource, not a certification that a particular workflow is compliant.

Trait	Description
Active When	Nobody can name who has the authority and understanding to stop a workflow before it becomes a dependency
Warning Signs	Teams cannot identify who can approve or stop a workflow; concerns linger because they sound too novel or too technical; governance documents grow while operational clarity does not; let's review it ends with a period
Damage Type	Unreviewed high-stakes workflows in production; accountability chains that terminate at a process, not a person; risks that compound silently until they become expensive
Summoned By	Control functions asked to evaluate what they cannot evaluate; leaders who confuse process with authority; teams moving faster than governance; organizations waiting for regulation to do their thinking
Feeding On	Process without authority; caution without action; review without decision; the assumption that someone else understands the concern better
Immunity To	Additional policy documents; more meetings; we take this seriously; waiting for the right moment
Vulnerable To	Named accountability for high-stakes decisions; authority assigned before the crisis; someone who can translate technical risk into business language and is empowered to act on it
Weakness	The moment someone asks who is the person, not who is the committee

Counter-Moves at a Glance

Role	Move	How It Lands
Legal	Authority Mapping	Names the person who can stop a workflow, not just the committee that reviews it
Security	Operational Stop Power	Ensures review means pause, not documentation while the system keeps running
Leadership	Pre-Crisis Assignment	Assigns decision authority before the emergency, not during it
Compliance	Translation Layer	Converts technical risk into business language that executives can act on

Part IV: Countermoves

This part moves from recognition to response. The mess cannot be eliminated. It can be noticed earlier, while the pilot is still a pilot and the plan is still a draft and the workflow still has an owner who can say no.

Chapter 12: Countermoves — A quick reference to the book's practical responses, organized by who has to make them.

Chapter 13: Conclusion: Read the Scroll Before You Cast It — The closing argument: generation got cheap, and none of the hard parts did.

By the end of this part, the reader should have a vocabulary and a few questions sturdy enough to survive the next planning cycle.

CHAPTER 12

Countermoves

Diagnosis is only useful if it changes how the party moves through the dungeon. Otherwise, you have purchased a more entertaining vocabulary for the same meetings.

The counter-moves in this volume are not glamorous. Most restore contact with reality before AI enthusiasm, generated prose, or vendor momentum hardens into infrastructure and habit. They include reading the proposal, counting the whole bill, and finding someone who can stop the system. You may feel these should already be happening. So did the people who approved the last rollout.

Every one appeared earlier in the book, next to the character or monster it answers. This chapter collects them so you can find them under pressure, which is when you will need them and when you will least want to re-read

Chapter 8. Pick the move that changes an actual decision. Forming a working group to evaluate the moves would give the monsters somewhere to sit.

The Moves

Move	Who makes it	The question to ask	Starves
Forecast at the scale of success	FinOps	"What does this cost if everyone loves it?"	Cost Singularity
Pre-commitment review	Leadership	"At what usage level do we redo the estimate, and who does it?"	Cost Singularity
Usage ring-fence	Engineering	"What is capped until the unit economics are proven?"	Cost Singularity
Follow the workload	FinOps	"What is the full cost to serve, across every cost center?"	Cost Singularity
Define success before the pilot	Product	"What metric, what threshold, by when, and what decision does it trigger?"	Cost Singularity, Backlog Engine
Run your own eval	Engineering	"Can we run this on our data, against our edge cases?"	Backlog Engine (via the Illusionist)
Keep two viable alternatives	Architecture	"What does it cost to leave?"	Cost Singularity (via the Enchanter)
Write the roadmap into the contract	Legal	"Can we add a date and a remedy?"	Backlog Engine (via the Bard)
Explicit exclusion	Product	"What are we explicitly not doing this quarter?"	Backlog Engine
Adopted by	Everyone	"Who read this and answers for it?"	Backlog Engine
Output versus outcome audit	Engineering	"What shipped, and did it solve the problem we selected?"	Backlog Engine
Named owner rule	Engineering	"Which person, not which team, owns this agentic workflow?"	Autonomy Mirage
Accountability chain audit	Leadership	"If this goes wrong, who explains it to the customer?"	Autonomy Mirage

Move	Who makes it	The question to ask	Starves
Synthetic-to-real ratio	Product	"How much of our customer understanding came from talking to customers?"	Autonomy Mirage
Action boundary review	Security	"What can a malicious prompt make this system do?"	Autonomy Mirage, Black Hole
Authority mapping	Legal	"Who can stop this workflow? Not who reviews it. Who can stop it?"	Compliance Black Hole
Operational stop power	Security	"Does review mean pause, or documentation while it keeps running?"	Compliance Black Hole
Enforcement behind every policy	Compliance	"What happens if a team skips this?"	Compliance Black Hole
Translation layer	Compliance	"Who here speaks both engineering and risk?"	Compliance Black Hole
Mandated dissent	Leadership	"Who disagrees, and who is not in the room to say so?"	All of them

Three Habits Under the Table

Treat expansion as a decision. Success does not imply rollout. Name who approves the larger commitment, what it costs, what it displaces, and what would trigger a review. A short written decision may be enough; the point is to make the choice visible. Otherwise the pilot expands because "a few more people asked," until those few people include every cost center and an external customer.

Evaluate on a schedule, not once. Repeat your own representative tests when a model, prompt, tool permission, or workflow changes, and periodically between changes. Record the version and configuration, the outcomes, the failures, and the cost. The vendor's benchmark is useful context. Your customer does not have a benchmark problem; they have the problem they called about. Include that one.

"Not now" is a selection, not a delay. "We are not doing this this quarter" is a choice. "We are doing this later" is a hope. Write down the exclusion and what new evidence would reopen it. Otherwise the rejected proposal comes back next month with “agentic” in the title, wearing the same shoes and pretending you have never met.

Make the Move Real

Put the cost beside the result. Take one workflow through a normal case and a messy one. Count the calls, retries, execution time, and reviewer effort required to reach an accepted result. Claude Code provides cost-management guidance; GitHub documents the usage charged by its coding agents.[49] Use the accounting path for your actual account. A subscription allowance, an API bill, and time spent repairing the answer are different things. They all belong in the same decision, even if procurement has helpfully arranged for them to arrive in different inboxes.

Give the owner something to own. In Linear, agent delegation leaves a human responsible for the issue.[50] Carry that distinction into whichever tracker you use. The owner should be able to explain the selected problem, accept or reject the result, and remove work that no longer matters. “Assigned to Claude” explains who is generating the pull request. It does not explain who decided the pull request should exist.

Test the refusal. In a sandbox, have the workflow propose an action it should not take. In Python, LangGraph's interrupts can pause a workflow for a decision. In TypeScript, Vercel's AI SDK includes tool-approval controls.[51] Wire the gate before the side effect, then verify rejection, timeout, restart, and attempts to use another tool to reach the same resource. The test should prove that the action did not happen. A beautifully worded apology is a failed test with good communication skills.

Keep the embarrassing examples. Turn failures and awkward edge cases into a small regression set. Promptfoo has guides for testing agents against unauthorized access, prompt injection, and other attacks, as well as integration with delivery pipelines.[52] Test your assembled application with safe fixtures, not just the model in an empty chat. Record what actually ran and inspect consequential actions. Passing one run is evidence about that run; repeating the difficult cases is how you learn whether the improvement holds.

---

[49] Anthropic, “Manage costs effectively,” Claude Code; GitHub, coding-agent usage costs. Documentation checked September 12, 2026.

[50] Linear, “AI Agents”, checked September 12, 2026.

[51] LangChain, LangGraph interrupts; Vercel, AI SDK tool approval, checked September 12, 2026. Verify the coverage of the actual execution path, including delegated work.

[52] Promptfoo, “How to red team LLM Agents” and red-team quickstart, checked September 12, 2026. A test tool helps gather evidence; it does not certify that a system is safe.

Do not quietly remove the case that keeps failing because it is "unrepresentative." It was representative enough to happen.

These tools are examples of mechanisms you can use. Installing all of them would also be a very efficient way to summon another backlog. Start with one workflow, a named owner, a budget boundary, and a demonstrated stop. Bring the result to the next review. Someone may still ask for a maturity model, but at least you will have something working while they explain the axes.

CHAPTER 13

Conclusion: Read the Scroll Before You Cast It

The easiest lie of the current AI era is that producing the thing was the whole job. Generation got cheap. Selection, ownership, and saying no remain expensive in all the ways a pricing page does not mention. Reading the thing before you ship it is, astonishingly, still hard. We can now produce a strategy in thirty seconds and spend two quarters avoiding the question it failed to answer.

That is true for code. It is also true for plans, budgets, dashboards, requirements, and policies. The Python runs. The TypeScript checks. The presentation has a sensible title and a concluding slide about next steps. None of that tells you whether the organization should be doing the thing. The monsters live in the gap between an answer that looks finished and a decision somebody has actually thought through.

Why These Are Harder Than the Volume I Patterns

The developer anti-patterns have a location. You can point at the Fighter who landed four thousand lines before lunch and have the conversation. The Cost Singularity is not one person's fault. The Infinite Backlog Engine is not one person's project. They accumulate from decisions that were easy to explain at the time: the pilot expansion was supportive, the unread plan was urgent, the unasked cost question would have made the meeting uncomfortable. Each explanation sounds reasonable until you put them together. The result is an incident review in which everyone followed their incentives and nobody can find the person who approved the outcome.

You cannot fix that just by finding someone to retrain. Change what the organization expects and permits: forecast before commitment, name ownership before rollout, select explicitly before the backlog fills, assign authority before the crisis, read before approving. These are ordinary management practices. They sound less exciting than an autonomous enterprise, but they have the advantage of being things you can do this week.

The Names Are the Product

Everything else in this book, the character sheets, the stat blocks, the artifacts with their little stat lines, is in service of making the names stick. "We have a Compliance Black Hole" gives the room a pattern to examine. "You are a Policy Paladin" gives HR a new phrase to look up. Use the names to describe what is happening, including your own contribution. They should make the conversation easier to have, not give you a fantasy vocabulary for calling a colleague useless.

The names also compress an observation that otherwise takes half a meeting to explain. "The Backlog Engine is running again" can lead straight to "what comes off the list?" That is useful. A slide ranking departments by monster severity would be less useful, although I accept that someone is probably generating one right now. The vocabulary should shorten the distance to a decision. If it creates another assessment program, the Engine has learned to read.

The Tools Will Keep Getting Better

Anthropic's 2026 experiment in building a C compiler in Rust is a real reason to take coding agents seriously.[53] It does not tell you whether the next generated project belongs in your company. The achievement and the decision are separate work. Rust has an ownership system; your organization still has to arrange its own.

Cursor, Claude Code, Codex, and the agents appearing in issue trackers will keep changing what teams can attempt. The names and limits on the plans will change too. The durable question is what you can now do well enough to be worth doing, including the work of checking it. You do not have to deny a technical advance to decline the twelve projects somebody proposed after reading about it.

Self-Implication

I have been asked whether this book is pessimistic about AI. I use these tools daily, and the things you can do with them really are fantastic. That is why the failure modes are worth taking seriously. Nobody needs a field guide to a tool they immediately stop using. The trouble starts with the ones good enough to make us stop checking.

I have caught myself doing several of these things. I have contributed to the Backlog Engine by generating a plan, accepting it with minimal reading because the prose sounded well-considered, and discovering months later that the plan was not a plan. It had headings. At the time, this seemed significant. I have felt the pull of the Autonomy Mirage, describing what a system might do in ways that sounded more settled than the system was. I have watched the Cost Singularity form around me and helped it along by not asking the cost question early enough to matter.

I have also been the inconvenient person, the one who asked about the cost trajectory in a room that had already decided. That contribution is not always welcome. Nobody says "thank you for making the transformation smaller," even when smaller is exactly what would save it. The Field Guide is trying to make those questions routine before asking them becomes a test of someone's courage or employment prospects.

[53] Nicholas Carlini, Anthropic, "Building a C compiler with a team of parallel Claudes", February 5, 2026. The report includes both demonstrated capabilities and limitations.

The Test

If this book works, you should be able to say "this is the Autonomy Mirage again" or "who adopted this?" and have it lead to a useful answer. If the room laughs first, good. Recognition is doing its job. Then someone needs to change the plan, check the bill, or stop the workflow. Agreement with the joke is not implementation of the counter-move.

Read the scroll. Forecast at the scale of success. Name the person. Decide what you are not doing. Make sure someone can stop the thing before it becomes the thing nobody is allowed to question.

And read the scroll yourself. The summary says it is excellent.

Acknowledgements

My wife Susan, my son Thomas, and my daughter Josephine deserve my first thanks for being patient with me while I disappeared for a few weekends to write this second volume.

I am also grateful to the engineering, finance, and operations leaders who shared their experiences navigating AI adoption at scale — too many conversations to list individually, but the patterns in this book owe a real debt to those discussions.

For the second volume specifically, I want to thank the early readers who flagged gaps and suggested additions. Your feedback made the FinOps and vendor sections substantially better than the first drafts.

Finally, I want to thank Mike Loukides again — his editorial instincts continue to improve everything he touches.

A Note on Methodology

This book is not academic research. It does not have a sample size, a control group, or a peer-reviewed methodology section. What it has is observation — years of it, across enough organizations, teams, and AI deployments that the patterns started repeating with uncomfortable regularity.

The failure modes described here emerged from my own experience working with engineering and operations teams navigating AI adoption, from conversations with engineering leaders managing cost and complexity at scale, and from watching the same dynamics play out independently in organizations that share nothing except the underlying pressures of organizational AI deployment. Some of the patterns crystallized during specific projects. Others accumulated gradually as I noticed the same sequence of decisions leading to the same category of trouble in contexts that had no connection to each other.

I did not set out to build a taxonomy. I set out to name the things I kept seeing, because naming them made them easier to talk about. The organizational NPC framework came as a natural extension of the developer archetypes in Volume I — the same impulse to compress recognizable patterns into memorable labels.

Where the book makes claims about prevalence — that certain organizational patterns are common, that they appear across different company sizes and technology stacks — those claims are based on pattern recognition, not quantitative measurement. I have tried to be honest about that throughout. When I say "I keep seeing this," I mean it literally: I keep seeing it. That is the evidence. It is the kind of evidence that practitioners have always used to build shared vocabulary, from Christopher Alexander's pattern language to the Gang of Four's design patterns to the anti-patterns catalog that inspired Volume I. None of those books came with datasets either. They came with recognition — the experience of reading a description and thinking, "I know exactly what that is."

If the patterns in this book match your experience, they are doing their job. If they do not, set them aside and name the patterns you are actually seeing. The vocabulary matters more than my particular version of it.

Glossary

Quick definitions for key terms and named entities in *The AI Developer's Field Guide, Volume II*. Use this as a quick reference when someone mentions a term in a meeting and you need the two-sentence version.

NPC Categories

FinOps. The financial operations category. FinOps practitioners connect technology spend to business value through usage visibility, timely data, optimization, and financial accountability. Their failure mode is control without judgment: reasoning from the current bill, overbuilding infrastructure, over-optimizing margins, hiding automation inside personal output, or letting dashboards tell a cleaner story than the numbers deserve.

Tokenomics. The newer discipline that follows AI economics from production to consumption to value: what a token costs, what a completed unit of work costs to serve, and what the work returned. Named and standardized by the Tokenomics Foundation (Linux Foundation, 2026). FinOps manages technology spend; Tokenomics refuses to stop at the token.

Architect. The explanation-layer category. Architects translate ambiguity into technical direction: conceptual approaches, system shape, technology choices, and the boundaries between generated output and human accountability. Their failure mode is authority without current evidence.

Vendor. The external-aspiration category. Vendors sell futures, package roadmaps as inevitabilities, curate benchmarks, and translate lock-in into convenience. The buyer's failure mode is dependency without bargaining power: they signed the contract before they understood what they were buying.

Infosec, Legal, and Control. The governance category. Security, legal, and compliance practitioners apply existing frameworks to AI systems. Their failure mode is control theater: documentation that satisfies auditors without reducing AI risk.

Executive. The leadership category. Executives fund the experiment, set the tempo, and decide what the organization announces. Their failure mode is buying confidence before the team has evidence, with the confidence now supplied by a model that never hesitates.

NPCs and Anti-Patterns

FinOps

slopcodex.com/bestiary/generic-finops

Avalanche Skeptic. Dismisses AI cost risk because the current bill still looks small. Forecasts by multiplying the pilot's bill by twelve. Signature line: "It's only API calls."

CapEx Knight. Insists the organization can build AI infrastructure cheaper in-house before the workload is known. Arrives with a utilization spreadsheet in which every cell says 95 percent.

Efficiency Evangelist. Cannot stop optimizing after the meaningful savings are gone. Trims 340 tokens from the system prompt and presents the eleven-dollar saving on a slide with a green arrow.

Ghost in the Ledger. Produces unusually strong FinOps work while hiding how much of it the model did. The forecast has a bus factor of one, and the bus is a spreadsheet.

Dashboard Necromancer. Can raise the chart that supports, stalls, or kills a project at exactly the right moment. The numbers are accurate; the graph answers a question nobody asked.

Architects

Agent Whisperer. Translates agentic AI possibility into organizational certainty by speaking about the near future in the present tense.

Legacy Laureate. Built something great somewhere else, long ago, and brings every current architecture conversation back to it. Charges a 30 to 40 percent meeting tax.

Last Stand Architect. Refuses to admit that AI can assist architecture or programming in any meaningful way. Skepticism hardened into refusal; the answer is known before the workflow is discussed.

Vendors

Vendor Bard. Sells not just a product but a historical threshold, converting market anxiety into social pressure. Signature move: making *not buying* feel like cowardice.

Friendly Familiar. Builds personal affinity until the buyer mistakes a friendly relationship for aligned incentives. Shared interests earn the vendor a meeting; they do not make the product pass an evaluation.

Purveyor of Doom. Presents the vendor's product as both a looming catastrophe and an essential purchase. A sincere warning can still serve a commercial incentive.

Benchmark Illusionist. Curates benchmarks that flatter the product. The numbers are real in a narrow sense and irrelevant in the broad one.

Lock-In Enchanter. Wraps dependency in soothing language: you are not trapped, you are standardized. Convenience becomes infrastructure one reasonable choice at a time.

Proprietary Vocabulary Mage. Renames familiar capabilities until branded vocabulary replaces comparison. Ask what the feature does, what limits it has, and whether another tool can do the same work.

Infosec, Legal, and Control

Compliance Oracle. Consulted when a workflow is already in use and the compliance question is still undefined. Rarely says yes, rarely says no, speaks in conditional blessings. Signature line: "Based on the information provided..."

Policy Paladin. Protects the organization through policy accumulation. Version 7.3.2 now defines "semi-autonomous synthetic decision support." Whether the policy stops anything is a separate question.

Terms Warden. Reads vendor terms the way a dungeon keeper reads old curses: carefully, literally, and usually after someone has picked up the glowing artifact. Signature line: "The slide deck is not the agreement."

Data Gatekeeper. Tracks where the data goes and who touches it. Serene because the database was never exfiltrated; missed the part where an agent was talked into deleting it.

Executives

Warlock of Staff Reduction. Frames every AI initiative by what it replaces rather than what it enables. Equates human labor with token volume. Signature line: "This agent can handle what three people do today."

Court Sorcerer. A yes-man with a model. Feeds the executive's preferences into the system and returns them as strategy, with citations.

Solo Sovereign. Has confused personal throughput with organizational impact. Implements every idea the team proposes before the team can, then interprets the resulting silence as agreement.

Befuddled Monarch. Uses infinite analysis to avoid ever having to choose. Signature line: "I'm still gathering information."

Strategy Improviser. (Sub-pattern, Chapter 9.) Generates a strategic direction in the moment it is needed and treats the generation as a substitute for developing a position through experience and argument.

Monsters

Cost Singularity. Appears when AI spend compounds faster than the organization can explain, govern, or connect to value. Feeds on pilot-scale assumptions, broad adoption, long contexts, hidden usage, and the word "pilot" after it stops being accurate. Weakness: someone asking what happens if people actually like it.

Infinite Backlog Engine. Appears when AI-accelerated generation outpaces prioritization, design, and review. The cost of proposing collapsed; the cost of deciding did not. Weakness: someone asking what was decided and why.

Autonomy Mirage. Appears when agentic output is treated as equivalent to responsible human action. The organization speaks in a grammar of action without a grammar of responsibility. Weakness: "Who decided this was good enough to act on?"

Compliance Black Hole. Forms when governance exists as process but not as assigned authority. Everyone agrees the workflow should be reviewed; nobody can stop it. Weakness: "Who is the person, not the committee?"

Artifacts

Forecast of Comfortable Linearity. (Dashboard Necromancer.) Last quarter's spend drawn into next quarter with a ruler. Extrapolation with a font.

Ledger of Justified Enormity. (CapEx Knight.) A large AI program rendered as a list of reasons it must continue. Every line defensible; the total not.

Unit Cost Abacus. (Efficiency Evangelist.) Counts tokens to the fourth decimal place and cannot tell you whether the system is worth running.

Pilot That Proved It. (Avalanche Skeptic.) Ten users, a friendly dataset, and a builder standing nearby, presented as proof that four thousand users with hostile data will also be cheap.

Amulet of Past Glory. (Legacy Laureate.) Gives every current AI problem a former employer, a former platform, and a story that begins before half the team had a LinkedIn profile.

Benchmark Scroll. (Benchmark Illusionist.) The most honest dishonest document in enterprise software. Every number accurate; none of them yours.

Roadmap Promise. (Vendor Bard.) A sincere statement of intent by someone who does not control the engineering schedule, hardening in internal meetings from "on the roadmap" to "when it ships."

Integration Web. (Lock-In Enchanter.) The accumulated SDKs, wrappers, and dependencies that make switching feel like surgery. Only visible from outside.

Inevitability Deck. (Vendor Bard.) Proves the category is transformational; says nothing about whether this product solves this problem. The window has been closing for eighteen months and will keep closing for eighteen more.

AI Governance V4.2. (Policy Paladin.) Thorough, cross-referenced, color-coded, and describing the systems the organization was deploying when it was written. Always 4.2, because 4.3 is waiting on Legal.

Vendor Questionnaire. (Data Gatekeeper and Terms Warden.) Real governance for the vendor who stores your data; silent on the vendor whose model decides things with it.

Retroactive Approval. (Compliance Oracle.) A seatbelt put on after the accident. Documents a decision the organization's behavior already made.

Terms of Service Nobody Read. (Terms Warden, who read them; everyone else, who did not.) The most important document in the vendor relationship and the least read. Those two facts are related.

slopcodex.com

You have the names. The field guide continues at slopcodex.com. The catalog is at slopcodex.com/bestiary.

Sign up for the newsletter there if you want new field notes, new names as they show up, and a note when something else in the series ships. There is also a card deck for people who want the taxonomy on a table: characters, monsters, artifacts, the whole bestiary as a physical reference.

Beyond the Slop Codex

The Slop Codex series is designed to entertain. The jokes, monsters, and bad habits also point to questions about AI, responsibility, and governance that I explore in two related works.

The Orchestrator is a work of nonfiction about directing AI systems and the human judgment that work requires. It develops some of the ideas and practical hints found throughout these field guides.

readorchestrator.com

The Condition Set is a series of fictional novels focused on AI and governance. It explores related questions through the people and institutions living with the consequences.

theconditionset.com

Index